Collins

Manual for missionaries
on furlough

Manual for
MISSIONARIES ON FURLOUGH

Marjorie A. Collins

533 HERMOSA STREET • SOUTH PASADENA, CALIFORNIA 91030

Library of Congress Catalog Card Number 72-92747
International Standard Book Number 0-87808-119-4

Published by the William Carey Library
533 Hermosa Street
South Pasadena, California 91030

Second Printing 1978

In accord with some of the most recent thinking in the academic
press, the William Carey Library is pleased to present this
scholarly book which has been prepared from an author-edited
camera ready copy.

PRINTED IN THE UNITED STATES OF AMERICA

Dedicated to

KAREN I. ADAMS

who, being a new creature in Christ,
is a challenge to me,
not only in her growth in grace and knowledge of Him,
but in her cheerfulness, discipline,
and desire to serve Him.

Contents

Dedication

Preface

Preface

A missionary on furlough! It hardly seems possible that you have been on the field for a term. So much has happened. You have changed and matured. You remember when you were younger and listened to missionaries tell of their fields and their work. Little did you realize the experiences through which God had actually led these folks. But now you are standing where they once stood. You've gone through your years of training, the struggles of finding the Mission of God's choice for you, the initial acceptance and orientation, followed by deputation and that happy day when you were, at last, on your way to the field.

You've completed a term or more of service, and you're a missionary in good standing. People will respect you and seek you out. You will have an opportunity to speak on many platforms, in many groups, and to countless individuals. You will share your life and work with interested people from many walks of life and at all levels of spiritual attainment. You will have an opportunity to challenge multitudes with the privilege of serving the Lord.

But furlough is not merely a time for public appearances. It is a time of reflection, refreshment, rest and renewal; of evaluating the past and setting goals for the future; of personal rededication to the service of Jesus Christ.

All too soon the days in the homeland will pass, and you will be on your way back to the field once more. God bless you, each one, during this furlough time, and may your next term of service be mightily blessed of Him in the strengthening of your own faith as well as in the privilege of sowing the Word and thus helping to strengthen others. He has given you this responsibility of ministering in His Name "for the perfecting of the saints, for the work of the ministry, for the edifying of the body of Christ." (Eph. 4:12). To what greater work could an individual devote his life?

1

Reasons For A Furlough

Most of us have heard of missionaries who have "gone national", decided furloughs were not vital, and have, therefore, stayed on the field for exceptionally long periods of time. This used to be more popular when travel was not only expensive but extremely difficult; when men determined they would probably give their lives for the sake of the gospel; when full-time service was a 24-hour day, 7-day week, with no time for rest, family and the homeland. In some cases, missionaries still have these basic principles which they intend to carry out. But most pioneer fields are open today; Mission Boards have been set up to see that the needs of their missionaries are met in every way; one cannot get away from such niceties of life as the retirement fund, life insurance, health insurance, Social Security, and along with this comes the statement of the Board that furloughs must be taken every so many years. Why have they come to this conclusion? Let's consider some of the reasons:

1. To become renewed physically through medical attention and to obtain rest and a change of environment in order to preserve or restore health and energy.

2. To be refreshed spiritually in the homeland through Christian fellowship.

3. To be strengthened emotionally through contact with friends, family and supporters.

4. To seek a place of fellowship where you can be nourished by the Word of God and supported through prayer if your home church and close friends are far from you.

5. To evaluate what has been accomplished during your term of service.

6. To set goals for your next term of service.

7. To bring personal reports to your supporters.

8. To maintain and add support to your account.

9. To make your Mission, your field, and your work known as widely as possible.

10. To obtain a change of environment.

11. To obtain intellectual refreshment (through special work at college, university, seminary, radio or technical school, secular work, etc.)

12. To keep you in touch with trends in your specialty.

13. To keep you abreast of happenings in the homeland.

14. To allow your children to become acquainted with their home country and relatives.

15. To renew your acquaintance with casual supporters.

16. To interest others in joining you on the field under your Board.

17. To encourage churches and individuals in their responsibility to missions.

Some have felt it would save much money, confusion and time if furloughs were eliminated. This is very true. But on the other hand, as we look at the intensity of the service performed on the field and the drain on every supply within you, it would seem that a furlough is essential for the best spiritual, physical, mental, social,

psychological and emotional health to be maintained
properly. And without this balance, missionary service
will be fruitless and discouraging.

It is interesting that soldiers and missionaries
are both given furloughs. And as good soldiers of Jesus
Christ, His servants need this departure from the things
which are so daily on the field, and the problems
and heartaches which are faced, in order to return to
the battle and "fight the good fight of faith". You
owe it to your Lord, yourself, your constituency and
your Mission Board to take advantage of this opportunity
given to you of renewing your mind, strength, soul and
body.

You'll be amazed at how problems become small when
seen from a distance and in a right perspective. You
become prepared to return to those servants, those unbe-
lievers, those troublemakers, those difficult co-workers,
with a new slant on the situation. It might even be
possible for you to determine how you may be able to fit
better into the total situation - to take orders, to
give orders; to discipline, to be disciplined; to organize;
to get the job done with less tension; to give credit
where credit is due; to allow the nationals their right-
ful place, etc.

Having returned to your homeland, you may come to
realize that the problems and disadvantages of the mission
field are not nearly so great as you had imagined them
to be. Trying to fit into the home situation will often
make your call to the field more pronounced and needy.
When you weigh both sides of the matter you may discover
how wonderfully God has prepared you for your task.

A furlough is a time for evaluating your entire
missionary calling and work, and seeing it in its proper
connotation. If you had your life to live over again,
what would you have done with it? May God impress upon
you the fact that given another opportunity to choose
your life's career, you would be compelled by Him to
become a missionary.

If you were once assured of His calling, be sure you
are certain of His continued leading. Without a sure
knowledge of His directing, missionary work will be

fruitless, discouraging and a total loss to you and those to whom you go. So get this fact settled with Him during furlough. Then commit yourself to Him more fully than ever before for the work to which He will direct for your coming term of service.

2

Length Of Furlough

For most missionaries, we have seen the demise of the 6-year term of service. Most Boards give their missionaries an alternative such as:

2 years on the field and 3-4 months of furlough

3 years on the field and 8-9 months of furlough

4 years on the field and 1 year of furlough

And for varying reasons, missionaries are wisely choosing the plan which is most convenient for them, although the Board usually sets the time limit for the first term missionary. There are advantages and disadvantages for each choice. Let's consider a few:

1. Two years on the field and 3-4 months at home.

ADVANTAGES	DISADVANTAGES
No need for missionaries to be moved to your station to take over your work, and perhaps continue on after your return so you are forced to go to a new station.	Often a missionary takes over your work as well as keeping up with his own so the work drags along until your return. Or a short-term replacement, whose heart is not with your people, may be sent.

For parents with chil-
dren, there may not have to
be a transfer to schools in
the homeland for the short
time at home since the furlough would normally come
during school vacation.

Some cooler countries have
their long school vacation
in mid-winter, the hardest
time for parents to leave
their work.

In some cases, older children will be left on the
field in school while the
parents take a brief fur-
lough.

Children may wish to go
to the homeland with their
parents and they should be
encouraged in this.

Air travel makes every
country close to the
homeland.

Travel home every two years
can become a heavy finan-
cial burden to you and/or
your Mission.

It keeps your supporters
much more up-dated on your
activities.

New slides, movies, other
audio-visuals and new
methods of presenting the
work must be utilized
to keep your reports interes
ting. This is more difficult for those not adept
at speaking.

You will be able to get
away from your work in
order to evaluate it and
plan goals for your return.

If you have been on the
field only one term of
2 years, you may have just
finished language study and
have not really adjusted
to the field. (Thus some
missions give a choice of
length of service only after
the first term).

Supporters and relatives can
be visited and since the
short furlough is almost
always taken in the summer
months, there is opportunity
to attend Bible Conferences.

If supporters and relatives
are spread across the countr
there may not be opportunity
to visit all of them, and
very little time to present
the work of the mission for
other than obtaining or mair
taining support. Most of tl

There will be openings to attend camps and DVBS programs for sustained emphasis upon your field.

time will be spent in travel with little or no time to rest.

It is more difficult to obtain deputation meetings during the summer "slump" in homeland churches and missionary conferences are usually scheduled for spring or fall. Although you may be able to speak in churches where pastors are on vacation, it is always better to speak where the pastor is present so that he can later direct the church in giving and concern for you.

Short term projects can be planned and consummated on the field, thus giving a feeling of accomplishment and success.

Long-term projects cannot be completed before furlough. Unless someone else has your zeal for and interest in it, they can fail.

2. 3 years on the field and 8-9 months at home.

ADVANTAGES

DISADVANTAGES

This gives you enough time to see your programs put into action and to plan for their supervision.

Very few programs can be implemented in such a short time. You may try to extend yourself too far to complete certain projects before furlough.

Your travel support is not as hard-pressed to be replenished.

If you have a large family, it may be difficult to raise this extra travel money every 3 years.

Your first term will see you having "learned" the language and gotten a start into your own work.

You may only have been on a station for a year or less before having to leave, depending on the length of time committed to language study.

It allows time enough to visit friends, relatives and supporters even if they are far-removed from one another. It should also provide for at least 2 months of rest, relaxation, rehabilitation and goal setting. It will also give an opportunity to be home for the "family" holidays (Thanksgiving, Christmas, New Years).

It often does not provide sufficient opportunity for taking educational techni- cal or professional courses which could be valuable for your ministry.

It can give the children a summer at home and a semester of school so they are not completely out of touch with what is going on in the homeland.

Since missionary schools are unusually advanced, a child may be put in a higher grade in the home- land, causing some frustra- tion and many adjustments with the result that he "wastes" his semester of study in the homeland.

3. 4 years on the field and 1 year at home.

ADVANTAGES

DISADVANTAGES

You become completely en- gaged in your field work with less attention on packing, unpacking, moving, adjusting, settling in, etc.

You may feel the work on your station is too much "yours" and unintentionally forget the need for team effort.

It may allow you to settle into your own station for 2 or 3 years, thus becoming more fully acquainted with your people and your responsibilities.

You might be a better worker as an itinerant, or as a specialist or consultant moving to new situations every 2 years.

It further alienates you from the conveniences and material benefits which you relied upon in the homeland, but now find are not needed for efficient operation.

You may find it difficult to adjust to things as they are in the homeland, preferring the simpler life and thereby offending some of your friends and supporters.

It helps you to understand better your field authorities and your special niche in the work assigned.

It may, unconsciously, give you the feeling that an appointment giving you greater authority should be given upon your return from furlough, whether you are capable of it or not.

It puts you in a situation where your co-workers become your "family" with special joys and privileges.

Unfortunate situations can arise which cause bitterness and disappointment and may be the cause of a resignation from the Mission.

There is a wholehearted effort to put permanence into the work and to teach nationals responsibilities since someone else will probably be taking over your work for your year of furlough.

Nationals may not respect or respond to the one(s) who is (are) sent to carry on the work in your absence.

It gives you the privilege of taking a year of College work in your specialty, take refresher courses in education, medicine, engineering, mechanics, etc.

It may be that your course will take 2 years to grant the degree you are seeking. You, not wanting to work at it piecemeal, request a year's leave of absence, thus increasing the personnel problem on your field.

You have opportunity for at least 3 months of rest - perhaps 2 months at the beginning of furlough and 1 at the end.

For some, the extra time simply means extra work since they feel guilty about taking an adequate rest break.

You can enroll your children in a full year of school in the homeland.

Depending on the type and place of the school, it may be better to have the children obtain as much of their education as possible in a Christian School on the field. Christian Schools at home can be expensive.

You can visit supporters leisurely and make new contacts for yourself and your Board.

If a married man, this may mean a great deal of time away from your family.

You may be asked to be an Assistant Pastor, Youth Director, Child Evangelism worker, Church Secretary, or take other responsibilities or offices in the church for a year (Men's Club President, Circle Leader, etc.).

There may be apprehension about taking meetings or committing yourself to an office. With a year to spend at home, boredom can set in and questions will arise concerning the adviseability of returning to the field.

You may wish to work during furlough to learn up-to-date and efficient methods of doing your work on the field.

Work may involve you to such an extent and the salary look so profitable that the decision is made to continue working rather than returning to the field.

There is time to be with the family in relaxed and rewarding situations.

Children may be taken up with all that could be available to them if they were to stay home.

If there have been diffi-
cult problems on the field,
there is time to begin to
see them and the people
in proper perspective.

Too much time to dwell on
the past defeats may ad-
versely affect your eager-
ness to return to the
situation.

There is sufficient time
for those who have been
laid down with malaria,
dysentery, or other de-
bilitating illness to be-
come renewed physically
before return to the field.

You may have had a disease
striking at you for some
time, but insisted on com-
pleting your term of ser-
vice, thus delaying medical
treatment and thereby ex-
tending your physical
problem.

You will be able to add your own lists of advantages
and disadvantages. A great deal will depend upon the
type of work you are doing, where you are located, illness which may come upon you, whether you are single or
married, if you have school-age children or not, how
often you, personally, feel a need for a change such
as the homeland can provide, how well you have adjusted
to the field.

Other factors may also enter the picture. You may
want a 4-year term in order to take a year of furlough
to care for details concerning the adoption of a baby;
or you may find that you need a shorter furlough after
2 years in order to locate your aged parents into a
Nursing Home. Most missions today try to accommodate
the needs of their missionaries in these emergency and
unplanned circumstances.

It is, in any case, fair to give your Field Director
and his co-workers sufficient notice of your intention for
taking furlough. Plans must be made to fill the gaps.
You, yourself, will need approximately six months to get
things in order for a changeover of personnel, packing,
getting papers in order, and notifying home constituency
of your plans. This is especially important if you are
using the 2 years on the field with 3-4 months at home
plan.

If your Mission does not have a choice for you for
years of service and months of furlough, be assured that
they have determined a fair length of each for you. Have

confidence in their decision, and except in emergencies, do not ask to circumnavigate this rule.

You may be serving under a Board which works in many countries of the world. You may be tempted to question why your term is longer than that laid down for another area. Again, trust your Board. They have looked carefully into the situation and have tried to take all things into consideration before determining your length of service.

Other Missions in your field may have shorter or longer terms than you. They have their good reasons, too. If you think your Board is unfair in this matter, look into the situation very carefully before you condemn your Board. If there are injustices or inequities, and others feel this, too, your Board will be glad to communicate with you by letter or in person to see if the matter can be worked out.

If, during your term of service, you have married one who is from a country other than your own, it could well be the determining factor as to the length of your furlough. For example, consider a girl from the United States who marries a man from Australia. Will they visit one homeland during one furlough and the other homeland during the next? Will they decide on a longer term on the field, thus assuring six months at home in each country? Or will the year of furlough be chosen so three months can be spent in one country and 9 months in the other, thus assuring the children adequate schooling without a need for having to adapt to two totally different educational systems? These questions must be weighed carefully, and in the event your mission requires you to take only a 3-month furlough, there must be careful planning for the use of the time since support may be coming from both areas. An unwise and unhappy decision would be for each partner to go his own way for the three months. Except for emergencies arising in the family, this would be the least satisfactory solution to the problem.

Some missionaries have decided to stay in their "adopted" land - in a different area, or one close by - for their short furlough. Some have even volunteered to help other missionaries in various ways during those short months. But such a plan is often less than adequate for the good of both the missionary and his work.

3

Preparations From The Field

Preparations for return to the homeland should be made at least 6 months before leaving the field. Keep in mind that you will have at least 3 major responsibilities while on furlough, i.e. (1) to yourself; (2) to your prayer and financial supporters; (3) to your Mission.

Men in the Service are familiar with the R and R leave. You, a missionary, also need Rest and Rehabilitation. Although your home church or supporting church may request that you speak as soon as you get off the plane, unless you have chosen a very short furlough, try not to plan extended deputation schedules for your first two months at home. You will need that time to become adapted to the homeland, to visit loved ones, to obtain spiritual refreshment, and to settle into your "headquarters". If you are a single person, you may be moving about during furlough with no "fixed" address for the entire period. Couples with children are usually obliged to stay in one place to enroll the children in school. You will need to decide where you would like to settle to be closest to those whom you love, or those among whom you will worship, or in the area where your children will be attending school. This is a fairly complicated decision if father and mother have different homelands.

Some Missions locate housing for their furlough folks. Many supporting churches provide housing for

their missionaries. There are missionary communities
set up in various sections of the country. Arrangements for the use of these facilities must be made well
in advance of your arrival. The larger your family,
the greater will be your problem.

You will want to send a prayer and newsletter from
the field telling of your furlough plans, announcing
the times you will NOT be available for services. You
may plan, tentatively, what areas you will visit and
the approximate dates for being in that vicinity. You
may decide to put this tentative schedule in your prayer
letter.

You will look over the slides and pictures you
have taken on the field. You will begin to plan several
slide series for use in deputation. Put your slides
together. Are you missing some key shots? You've still
got time to get them. Try to think of the various
groups you will be reaching at home. Then make series
accordingly - for children, for young people, for
women's groups, for church services, for general audiences
(schools and civic organizations) and others. Unless you
expect to pass over your slides in gunshot fashion and
leave your audiences gasping for breath and wondering
what they saw, use between 40 and 80 slides per series,
depending upon your emphasis and how much you intend to
say. Perhaps you will want to make a taped narration
with background sounds from the field. Or you may prefer to speak in person when presenting your slides. You
may wish to tape material from the field to assist with
other presentations, however. The Muslim call to
prayer, the sounds of the marketplace, a group of children singing in their native tongue, the braying of
donkeys, the sounds of camel bells - you'll think of
hundreds of sounds you'd like to share with the folks
at home, or that you will enjoy, yourself, during furlough. (You will be surprised how homesick for the field
you can become during furlough).

Begin gathering little items to present to your
supporters. They deserve a token of your appreciation.
No matter how small the gift, make sure it is unique to
the country in which you serve. Some missionaries have
purchased postage stamps to be given to stamp collector
supporters. For 50¢ or $1.00, a lovely gift can be
given, even if most of the stamps are of the lowest de-

nominations. Coin collectors will appreciate a coin or
two from your country. Handwoven bookmarks are usually
an easily attainable, yet inexpensive, item. Wood
carvings, pictures, calendars, knick knacks of all
kinds and descriptions are available to you. Although
it appears to be a large expense, some trouble, and
perhaps an extra bag, curios for yourself and your
friends are worthwhile. You may wish to find inexpensive items which you can leave in homes where hospitality is extended to you on furlough. Even if you, personally, are not interested in these items, it is
courtesy to show your appreciation, and what better
way than giving a token from your mission field?

There will be several legal matters to be cared
for on the field to make sure your residence papers and
visaes are in order. In some lands you may wish to
obtain a "No objection to Return" paper from the local
Commissioner to help with your re-entry papers following furlough. Shots and vaccination will be brought
up to date. Tax matters will be cared for. Passage
will be arranged. But most of all, you will want to
be sure to prepare the way for one who may take over
for you during your absence, whether national or missionary. Matters for which you are personally responsible
will be cleared up by YOU. Don't leave your work in
a position that will doom it to failure after your departure. Don't make nationals so dependent upon
you, as a person, that they are unable to take direction
from another, or from the Lord.

You may wish to take 8mm or 16mm movies which can
be edited and spliced at home. Make sure that you
have recent material to present to your home constituency.
Historical material is one thing; up-to-date missionary
presentations are quite another!

You will probably have to provide displays during
the course of your stay at home. Be thinking of items
which can be used. Curios, food, newspapers in the
national language, a Bible and/or hymnbook, clothes,
lamps, decorations, children's toys, pictures in plastic
folders, etc., are all useful for this purpose. Plan
your display now and be sure you have all the items you
will need to make it effective. Unless you are working
with naked tribespeople, be sure to carry at least

one native outfit home with you to wear during special
meetings. It is often good to take a set of children's
clothing, since dressing children in these clothes for
a Sunday School or Young People's meeting can be
effective.

Some zealous missionaries go to no end of trouble
to capture giant spiders, scorpions, baby boas, and
other animals and insects, put them in formaldahyde,
and carry them from conference to conference. Let's
try to avoid this type of presentation! It may be,
however, that you, or your children, have been able to
build up a beautiful display of butterflies. This is
much less alarming for public meetings!

Be sure to look into the principles and practices
of your mission by reviewing its handbook, to find out
what your responsibilities will be during furlough.
Perhaps there are matters suggested therein which should
be cared for on the field.

If you are planning to study during your furlough,
be sure to make arrangements with the school and your
Mission well in advance.

If personal items are to be loaned or stored or
sold, begin to take care of these matters a month or
two ahead of your departure.

Prepare, to the best of your ability, the nationals
who work with you for the change in leadership which
will take place upon your departure.

Inasmuch as possible, help prepare your children
for the return to the homeland. Many of them will be
unhappy at the thought of leaving their friends on the
field. They must understand why it is necessary for
them to return to the homeland for a while.

If you are a missionary in the homeland, there may
be less need for complex advanced preparations for
furlough. But there will still be a gap in the ranks
during your absence, so it is essential that someone
take over your responsibilities, if possible. If a
full-time person is not available, someone should be
placed in a position of supervision as a counselor and

resource person. Furlough is no less necessary for
"home" missionaries than for "foreign" missionaries.

Don't let the anticipation of "going home" adversely
affect the remainder of your term on the field. True,
there is much to be done in preparation. Some will have
projects they will want to complete and it will mean
a grueling schedule. Others may feel they should
slacken off their work to prepare others for the im-
pending "hole" which will be left upon their departure.
(It's sometimes easy to think "Now they'll realize just
how much I've been contributing up until now").

Just one last reminder. Unless the Lord originally
led you out for only one term of service as a specialist
for a designated task, or you are on loan to a particular
mission or field for a term, or one of your children
has developed a disease or malfunction which doctors
tell you will need many years of treatment in the homeland, or you, yourself, have been diagnosed as one who
would benefit from a lengthy stay in the homeland,
never, never, NEVER decide just before furlough that
you are not going to return to the field. Making such
a decision amidst the problems and pressures of the
situation in which you are located can result in a
wrong choice which can be a life-long regret. You may
be discouraged, downcast and disgusted. You may have
seen others get the credit for your labors. You may
have had personal and legitimate gripes against your
fellow-workers. You may be unhappy with the area in which
you were placed. You may have expected to be put into an
administrative role, but no one realized your potential.
On the other hand, you may have been placed in a position
of leadership for which you felt completely unprepared
and inadequate. You may have struggled over lack of
finances. You may have had severe illnesses during your
term. The language may have proven to be a formidable
foe which you were not able to conquer. So you decide
to give it all up - and you prepare NOT to return to
the field. Have a conference with your Field Director
before you leave, sharing problems and looking for solutions. BUT DON'T MAKE A DECISION TO RESIGN WHILE ON
FOREIGN SOIL. Be patient just a little longer and do
your work as unto Him. Trust Him to keep you. There
would not be nearly so many "missionary casualties" if
decisions had been made after a time of rest, fellowship
and evaluation in the homeland.

4

Furlough Housing

Missionaries planning to be in the homeland for more than three months will, undoubtedly, have a problem locating in an area and a home that will meet their needs and fit their budget.

We are grateful that God has raised up, in these days, several furlough communities where folks can stay for a period of up to one year. Ordinarily, reservations must be made well in advance of arrival in the homeland, although on occasion a forced cancellation will allow you to be accepted. These communities are well situated, provide all conveniences and are comparatively inexpensive. The fellowship with men and women from other missions is stimulating. The joy of being closely allied with Christians with the same concerns as yours is strengthening. The social and spiritual environment is energizing and invigorating.

There are supporting churches which provide homes for their own furlough folks on a "first come" basis. These may be homes owned and maintained by the church, or apartments in members' homes which are made available for missionary use. This might not work in a church situation which supports only 2 or 3 missionaries, but if there are a good number of them, it would be likely that the home or apartment could be kept filled continually. If such is the case in your home or supporting church, be sure to notify them well in advance of your furlough as to when you will arrive,

how many and what ages your children are, and for
how long you would like to be accommodated. This is a
real ministry for churches which are able to provide
this service. Never take it for granted. Live in and
care for the home as though it were your own.

For those on short furloughs, relatives are usually
anxious to provide accommodations. Since they may not
have seen the children for some time, they (especially
grandma and grandpa) may enjoy having them for three
months. When your parents are physically able to take
on this responsibility, it is of tremendous help when
it is essential for both of you to go to meetings or
conferences, or extended meetings either near or far.
For single folks, there is usually little problem in
finding housing with relatives or friends.

Even for some electing a longer furlough, family
and friends may desire to have you make your headquarters with them. It will depend upon individual
circumstances whether or not this is the best arrangement for you.

Since housing is essential on furlough, you will
have given it a great deal of thought before leaving
the field. You will have prayed much concerning it and
it will have been mentioned in your newsletter so that
others might join you in the fellowship of prayer. God
is very apt to answer those prayers, so be prepared for
it! From unexpected sources, you may find God supplying
your need. A friend of a friend, an acquaintance of one
of your supporters, people you've never met before will
offer facilities fully adequate to meet your needs in
the area in which you desire to settle. God answers
prayer in remarkable ways. And if it seems hard to
believe, try to remember back to the last time you heard
of a missionary who had no place to live during furlough.

For some there may be a necessity to find a home in
the community in which you have decided to settle. You
may be staggered by the rents requested to accommodate you
But you will find something suitable, and the Lord will
supply that which is needed above the normal furlough
housing funds designated for that purpose each month.

It makes sense that you will want to be centered

somewhere near your supporting churches. If your relatives are in the same area, it makes it very handy. Or
if you are planning on furlough education, you will
live near the school, seminary, or university which
you plan to attend. If you are being assigned to work
with the Home Office in a special project, you will
locate near your Headquarters. For those who have
their support pledged through their Board or denomina-
tion and are sent on tour, there is no real crisis as
to where to settle since you will be travelling in
every corner of the homeland.

It is important to take into consideration the
choice of living in the city, the suburbs, or the
country. City living is, of course, most expensive
and for a family of six or eight it can prove entirely
prohibitive. Living in the suburbs will usually provide for good schools for the children, lower rents,
adequate transportation, Christian fellowship, somewhat less danger due to crime, a place to park your car.
Country living is much more relaxing and restful. But
there are few conveniences. Children may have to travel
long distances to school. Shopping may have to be done
several miles away and if the husband is using the car
for deputation, unless the mother can find a friend to
transport her, or a store willing to deliver, this
could become a problem, especially in the winter in the
north.

It is almost certain that the majority of furlough
folks who must provide their own housing live in the
suburbs, then. Apartment houses are being built by
the hundreds and are sometimes obtained at a good price.
Be sure, however, to find out about the lease. If you
have a 9-month furlough and the lease runs for a year,
you will probably be responsible for the extra 3-months
rent unless a special arrangement can be made.

The possibility of renting a mobile home should be
considered if the space provided is adequate. These,
although usually immobile, are often inexpensive and
comfortable. It means little or no material things must
be purchased to furnish it, they take little time to
clean, they cost little to heat and/or air condition.
Purchasing a trailer or mobile home is probably not a
wise choice since the resale value is inadequate considering the short time you will be using it.

Furlough housing may appear to be a formidable barrier, but be assured of God's awareness of your need. And once again you will find that where He guides, He WILL provide.

5

Culture Shock

Culture shock was expected when you left the homeland for Language School or your term of service on
the field. You were, if not wholly ready for it, at
least mentally aware that your new environment would
provide a total change in standards, values, language,
culture, customs, etc. The actual shock level was determined by you, individually, and by the place to
which you were sent. Some folks adapt rather easily
to change; others are totally alarmed by it. Fortunately,
most missionaries find themselves somewhere in the middle
area, perhaps not fully acclimated to the new situation,
but at least able to cope physically, mentally, emotionally, socially and psychologically with that by
which they are surrounded.

Now you have been on the field at least a year -
perhaps as long as five years - and you are beginning
to enjoy your new type of living. You have learned to
communicate in the language of the people; you have
discovered that there is a certain sense of serenity in
the slower pace; being late no longer bothers you; if
something doesn't get done today, there is always tomorrow;
the sight of raw meat or fish hanging on the roadside
has become commonplace; the pungent smells of the marketplace are enjoyed; the lack of a sewerage system is over-
looked; the daily hassle with servants is a less tense
chore; the lack of privacy no longer troubles you;
fellowship with "foreign" Christians, like yourself, is
less needed; sharing with national believers and enter-
ing into their joys and sorrows has become an enjoyable
experience.

But now it is time for furlough. You have looked
forward to it with a great deal of anticipation. Going
home is a happy occasion for you will be getting some
needed physical rest and spiritual renewal, meeting
again with relatives and friends, and sharing your work
with supporters and other groups. You've had some
difficult situations to handle on the field; inter-
personal relations have often been strained even among
your own fellow-workers, both missionary and national;
financial trials have come again and again; sickness
has taken its toll; there have been frustrations on
every hand in spite of some evidence of advance in the
work and joy in service; you've missed having celery
and olives on the dinner table because they were too
expensive or unobtainable; you're tired of ghee in
place of butter; you wonder how your cook can make the
food so spicy hot; it will be good to speak your
mother tongue all the time; the children are also
anxious to get home.

But now you've just arrived on home soil. All of
a sudden you decide you had never realized the full
impact of culture shock. You expected it when you went
to a strange situation, but you never anticipated it
to be even more forceful as you return to the homeland.
True to form, things have been changing rapidly at
home. You've tried to keep posted on news, but you
realize you're out of touch. Relatives are happy to
see you, but even they are not quite the same as when
you left them. How were you to know that single-
breasted suits were out, wide ties were in, long dresses
were in, spike heels were out, etc. Styles change too
rapidly for a missionary to keep up with them. Or perhaps
you laughed at the clothes some kind person or church
sent you to make you presentable upon arrival. You
grimaced when you saw the violet shirt and mottled green
trousers, or the granny gown with long sleeves trimmed
with lace. But when you got off the plane and saw the
crowded terminal, you felt you were the only one wearing
clothes in style - the style you remembered from four
years before. When you get to the automobile which has
come to pick you up, you ask if you can drive and you
almost die of fright driving in traffic to which you are
entirely unaccustomed . . eight lanes of it heading out
of the airport . . and all driving on the "wrong" side
of the road. You had forgotten that driving on the

"other side of the road" had become as natural as breathing. You see the people surrounding you. Did they look like that when you left? Could there have been so many cults, sub-cults and mini-societies when you were home before? And on and on it goes. You are amazed at buildings and homes being razed in the city to make room for larger apartment buildings and condominiums. There is construction everywhere - new housing areas, model cities, urban renewal, roads, bridges. You can't even find your way around.

You aren't home long before you see how materialism has spread. The black and white TV is obsolete and at least one 21" color set is a minimal necessity of life. Each family must have two cars - and if there are teen-agers old enough to drive, there are apt to be more. You can't get into the rush of life in the homeland. You go to the store for a pint of ice-cream and discover 120 different flavors. The supermarket leaves you breathless. Every item seems outrageously expensive. Choices abound; decisions must be made quickly. Computers are doing the work you used to do in the company. You visit to say hello to your former boss, but he's been promoted and transferred to a locality 1500 miles away. You walk through the section where you used to be employed. Very few recognize you. The few who do are not very interested in you. But they are keen on showing you the progress they and the company are making. No one had written since they gave you that going away party, and everything you see is new to you.

Surely in your supporting churches - and in your home church - you will find stability. You've never met the new pastor who came shortly after you went to the field. You find the educational program highly organized. The church people have meetings of one sort of another every night of the week. Along with TV, sports and social obligations, it has drawn families apart so they can no longer plan even one night a week together. It is difficult for them to fit you into their schedule for a meal. You are anxiously willing and waiting to share your field experiences with them, but they are seemingly occupied with their own problems and involvements. There isn't much time for them to spend with you, and your desires for fellowship and sharing, to which you had looked forward so long, are quenched. Then, too, your friends

use words you don't understand. They tell jokes that
are meaningless. They speak of events, important to
them, of which you have not heard because you have had
no television, radio, newspaper or magazine on the
field.

And you begin to realize that you are suffering
from culture shock now as you never did when you went
to the field. You are finding it most difficult to
adjust.

Your children will face kinds of problems you had
never even thought of on the field. Their culture shock
will depend on how old they were when they left the
homeland, how much they remember of it themselves and
how much you have told them about things "back home".
The school system will have changed. Should they go to
a public or Christian School? How involved should you
allow them to become in social activities? In an age
when dating starts extremely early, where attendance at
"good" movies is not only condoned but encouraged, where
drugs are as easily obtained as a glass of water, where
permissiveness is rampant, where children are almost
undisciplined – what are the right answers? And when
other children have every material thing they desire,
how do you handle the matter of providing things for
your own? What about clothing crazes? Music fads? And
if your young child was born on the field, he may be
frightened by the "foreigners" surrounding him. Can he
be expected to "fit right in?"

You had expected to come home for rest and fellowship, renewal, revitalization, sharing, and a bit of
appreciation. But you are lost in the rushing crowd.
You've only been home two weeks, but already you are
looking forward to your return to the field. You are
lonely for your friends out there. Some of them, on
occasion, actually needed you. Things were so much
simpler and less expensive. They miss you, too. You'd
love a dish of hot curry, or injera and wat. So often
you open your mouth to speak your new language, but no
one here would understand. Yet it is so much more ex-
pressive. Satan, many times, tried you to the utmost on
the field. But he is no less challenging at home.

You go to the Lord and beg Him to give you strength

for these furlough days, to give you wisdom in talking with people, to give you a ministry that will be rich and rewarding, to give you adaptability for the changes you face, to give you discernment in dealing with your own family. Culture shock has been met head-on in the homeland, and you were entirely unprepared for it.

But God will help you through it. Trust Him for it, and remember to pray for those who continue to hold the ropes at home. They find it difficult to live an uncompromising and consistent Christian witness. Stand behind them in prayer even as they attempt to stand behind you. Perhaps you hadn't known how to pray for them any more accurately than they had known how to pray for you.

Whether this is your first furlough or your fourth, you will discover culture shock will be awaiting your arrival. You may not be able to adjust to it fully, but it is there, nevertheless, and you must be prepared to reckon with it.

6

Rest And Rehabilitation

"I don't have time."

"I don't need any."

"If I relax, I may never want to work again!"

"How can I?"

"I must see my supporters right away."

"I'm not being paid to rest."

"The Mission expects me to do deputation work."

"My account is in the red. I've really got to work hard to gain additional support."

"I'm too young to slow down."

"It's sort of a compulsion, I guess. I just don't feel right about resting for a month."

"I'm not really sick. I just feel tired."

And with these and a hundred similar statements, missionaries home on furlough rush here and there, filling their days and weeks with work and worry and return to the field less rested than when they arrived home. And some never make it back to the field for a second term because they have pushed their physical or emotional capacities to the limit and their health does not permit them to return.

One of the basic reasons for a furlough is for physical readjustment and rehabilitation. It is an important reason and should be considered very carefully by each individual.

Very few missionaries find their first term of service restful. There is too much adjustment to be made. Days are full of language study, work, people. Nights are short. Illness may have taken its toll. And yet when they arrive home, they find they are in high gear, and it is difficult to rest and relax. Perhaps there have been serious problems on the field and keeping busy at home helps to ease the intensity of them.

Rest does not imply sleeping 24 hours a day for a month. This is seldom helpful or necessary unless a person is deeply depressed and wants to block out the world around him. Usually two or three days when you can lie down any time and have no responsibilities is sufficient to begin the process of rehabilitation. This does not mean, however, that you are now ready to go on tour and speak in every church in the country with no further time for rest. Twiddling one's thumbs appeals to very few, but how about a week at a Bible Conference with no responsibilities? Or a week visiting friends in the old home town with no formal meetings planned? What's wrong with a week or two of vacation at the seashore, in the mountains, or camping? You've been collecting stamps in your country. Why not put them in order and enjoy them?

What we are really trying to avoid is a mad dash into deputation work with no preparation and no time to evaluate your term of service. Until you do this, you cannot properly challenge people or give them a balanced view of your work.

This should be a time when the Word of God and prayer become very real to you. Much time should be spent in the presence of God, seeking direction for your furlough months and committing it all to Him, for in this ministry as in all other phases of Christian living, without Him you can do nothing.

Perhaps it is absolutely impossible to arrange for a time of rest as soon as you reach the homeland. This does not excuse you from finding a time as soon as possible after your arrival for this. And days of travel between meetings cannot be considered a substitute. Nor can Monday and Tuesday do it in the event you have meetings on Sunday and Wednesday. You must set a time aside when you have no other responsibilities – just to enjoy life and do things you *want* to do. This is not being selfish; it's being sensible. Test yourself. See if even a week with no missionary responsibilities doesn't restore a serenity to you which you haven't known for quite a while. And it's amazing how different things appear to a relaxed mind in comparison to the way they appear to a tense, tired one. People and things begin to take on new meaning and perspective. Remember that God is no slave driver. He is not yet in the business of striking people dead for taking a day of rest.

Some of you with children will begin to realize how little time you've actually been giving to those little ones. No, your work didn't come before your children. Or did it? Give them some time now. Help *them* to rest, too. Give them time to adjust to their new situation. Let them unwind. Let them be normal children.

If you are single, you have no excuse for not resting. You will have far fewer demands upon your time than married folks. Or if you're planning on schooling during furlough, plan to arrive before school opens to give you an opportunity to become physically and mentally prepared for the days ahead. (If you have been away from formal studies for any length of time, you will be amazed at the change which has entered the academic world during recent days. This, too, will take a great deal of adjustment).

You will find the end of your furlough time will be hectic. Try to plan very carefully so that shopping, shots and social calls can be completed at least two weeks before your return to the field. This will give you some time to relax once again before returning to the field. Most missionaries say during furlough, "I'll be glad to get back to the field and get some rest," especially just before they are due to return. It ought not to be this way. Why should a missionary exhaust every resource during the time he is supposedly building himself up for another term?

There are many reasons, of course. Poor planning, demands by supporting churches, lack of sufficient support, and mission obligations are among them.

It is common knowledge that a sick missionary can hinder as much as help the work. If you came home with dysentery, malaria, or other tropical disease or para-site, unless you are rehabilitated, you are a poor risk for return to the field. Getting well is a priority consideration. Even getting your support level improved makes little difference if the mission doctor refuses to pass you physically. Rest and rehabilitation, there-fore, are of utmost importance. Take every opportunity you can find to renew your spirit, soul, mind and body. It is not wasted time. It is imperative. Even those who feel they can get by very well by pushing them-selves night and day on the field and at home will find, under careful analysis, that problems are becoming "muddy", decisions are not as quickly and keenly made, inter-personal relations are not what they once were. Age is blamed for a quick temper and impatience. Every-thing and everyone gets blamed when the real culprit is lack of rest and relaxation. So rest your body. Rest your mind. Rest your emotions. You'll be a different person, and far better for it.

7

Ask Yourself Some Questions

A good reason for the furlough period is to take an objective look at ourselves, our work, and our relationship with God and our fellow man. An evaluation of where we have been and a goal for where we are going is of the utmost importance if our lives are to be effective and fruitful in the total ministry committed to the church of Christ. It will also help us to determine our own strengths and weaknesses, giving us an opportunity for readjustment and change where it will prove beneficial.

Perhaps we should have entitled this chapter "Active Learning". We often think of learning as "that which we receive through instruction." But it is a far more active process than that. Some of its other meanings are "to find out", "to acquire knowledge or skill", to "ascertain", "to come to know", "to come to know how", "to fix in mind", "to acquire". Although education tends to take a more formal pattern, learning takes place constantly.

We do not intend to give specific answers to the questions which will be asked in this chapter. But if each of you, in the quietness and honesty of your own heart, will take several hours, or days, to find your *own* answers, you will be assured of a fuller knowledge of yourself, a better understanding of others, and more impetus for effective planning for your coming term of service.

A.　PERSONAL CONSIDERATIONS

　　1.　How satisfying is my devotional life?

　　　　Of what does it consist?

　　　　What could be done to make it more effective
　　　　　and meaningful?

　　2.　How long has it been since I've set down on
　　　　　paper my personal doctrinal statement?

　　　　Have there been any changes in recent years?

　　　　Am I over-emphasizing one doctrine and
　　　　　neglecting others?

　　　　Are there some doctrines which have become
　　　　　meaningless to me?

　　3.　Have I reread my mission's policies and
　　　　　practices?

　　　　Do I still accept and adhere to them, or do
　　　　　I rebel at some of them?

　　　　How does my rebellion come out?

　　　　Have I talked these matters over with my
　　　　　mission leaders?

　　4.　Do love, friendliness, respect, admiration,
　　　　　generosity, encouragement and sympathy rule
　　　　　my personal life and witness?

　　5.　Do I ever have a feeling of rage, fear,
　　　　　frustration, suspicion, being rejected,
　　　　　thwarted, withdrawal, despair, greed,
　　　　　anxiety, hate?

　　　　How do I handle these attitudes?

　　　　How do they handle me?

　　　　What do I do to alleviate the results of these
　　　　　attitudes?

Can they be changed?

Do I want them to be different?

6. Do I feel I really have nothing to offer and therefore am not worth much?

    Do I always allow my plans and ideas to be overridden because I'm afraid to speak up?

    Am I insecure in my attitudes concerning my own strengths and weaknesses?

    What *are* those strengths and weaknesses?

    What have I been doing with them?

    How much ego-strength do I have?

7. Do I go around in a false state of humility, degrading my natural abilities, feeling there is nothing positive which can come from me because "in me dwells no good thing?"

    Do I hide all strengths of my own in order that He might increase and I might decrease?

    Do I feel it is wrong to be able to do something well and admit it?

    Or, on the other hand, am I proud of what I am able to do?

    Am I sure of my ability to carry out my job?

8. Am I enthusiastic about my work or has it become something I *have* to do?

    Would I be better suited for something or somewhere else?

    Would I be more enthusiastic if certain changes were instituted?

    What changes?

    How can this be accomplished?

9. Am I optimistic in my outlook on life in general, and especially concerning my own problems?

   Or does pessimism creep into every thought I think and statement I make?

   Which is the healthier attitude?

   How can I begin to see the silver lining in the clouds?

10. Am I ready and willing to be flexible in my thoughts, in my work, in all of my relationships?

    Do I willingly offer to go or be or do, and then become very critical because I have been asked to go or be or do?

    Am I subject to jealousy?

    Am I proud?

11. Am I honest with myself?

    Have I correctly analyzed my feelings and the reasons for them?

    Have I covered up an attitude, a sin, an action, a decision, with a Scripture reference taken out of context?

    If I hate or fear something or someone, do I admit it to myself and face it for what it is, or do I cover it over because "Christians are not supposed to have those feelings"?

12. How do I face loneliness?

    Do I determine that Jesus is the only friend I ever need, and therefore suppress my feelings of aloneness?

    Or do I face the fact I am lonely and try to find my own answer for it?

13.   Do I find a critical spirit within me?

Do I feel my answers are usually best when questions arise?

Do I find myself criticizing everyone and everything?

How can I deal effectively with criticism?

Do I feel others are criticizing me?

What does this do to me?

What is my reaction?

How do I treat people whom I think are critical of me?

Am I easily hurt?

14.   How do I react to sickness?

Do I feel it is a weakness which must be overcome?

Do I follow doctor's orders?

If rest is required, do I rest?

Am I too busy to treat "minor" illnesses?

Do I "keep going" as long as possible without admitting to sickness so as not to involve family or co-workers?

Does physical sickness make me draw closer to the Lord, or does it produce a lethargy with the result that I feel others can uphold me in prayer because I don't feel able to maintain spiritual strength through my own efforts?

Is this a wrong attitude?

How do I react when co-workers become ill and demand time and attention I feel should be given to "serving the Lord"?

15. When pressure comes in upon me, how do I react?

    Do I become flustered, incommunicative, "up tight", irrational?

    Do I handle it as it comes and thereby maintain a normal boiling point?

    Do I feel pressure comes because of a lack in me or in my spiritual life?

    Does this become an opportunity for growth in grace, or depression and indecision?

    Do I blame other people for pressure?

    Do I cause some of it myself?

16. How do I really feel about the lack of privacy afforded me?

    The interruptions when I'm studying or resting?

    Do I enjoy having people stare at me like an animal in a zoo?

    Does it bother me that I can never get away from people?

    Do I have an open door policy?

    Should I consider closing that door at times?

    Do I really want nationals to feel free to come to me 24 hours a day for counsel and Bible study?

    Or do I inwardly rebel, but say nothing?

    Do I feel I am being exploited?

    Where and when do I feel I should be allowed privacy?

    Would privacy help my ministry to such a degree that I should demand it at all times?

17. How much appreciation do I feel I deserve?

    How do I feel when others get credit for what I have done?

    Is my feeling stronger in this regard if another missionary gets the credit, or if a national gets it?

    Can I continue happy in my work without being patted on the back constantly? Occasionally?

18. How creative am I?

    Am I happy doing the same thing the same way all the time?

    Could it be done differently?

    Could I put new interest and life into my work with a little creative effort?

    Is there someone who could help me with this?

19. How do I feel about money which I have?

    Do I cling to it and use it only for myself?

    Do I tithe and give gifts to the Lord?

    Do I share in needy projects?

    Is my pocketbook entirely the Lord's or do I pretty much hold the pursestrings?

    Am I generous, or do I withhold?

    Could I be considered careful in money matters?

    Am I "tight"?

    Am I "stingy"?

    Do I envy others who seem to have more than I do?

    Am I grateful for His continuous supply?

20. Am I a leader?

    Do I have administrative qualities?

    Am I decisive?

    Do I consider the needs of others in an unbiased way?

    Do I lead with authority? Democratically? Autocratically?

    Do I listen with an open mind?

    Do I consider every facet of a problem before making hasty decisions?

    Do I hedge?

    Do I try to push decisions off on someone else?

    Do I join the majority even if I am otherwise minded?

    Do I lead wisely with discernment?

    Do I try to be fair and just in all my dealings?

    Are there things I don't like to do? Refuse to do? Why?

    Am I loved and respected? Only loved? Only respected?

    Should I consider continuing in a leadership position, or should I step down and give someone else the responsibility if he is more qualified?

    What are my feelings when a *less* qualified individual assumes my place of leadership?

21. Am I a follower?

    Am I critical of the authority of my leaders?

    Do I respect those over me?

Do I try to make my leader's job easier by conferring with him periodically, keeping him posted on problems and happenings as seen from my viewpoint?

Do I openly talk against the leadership personnel?

22. Am I dependable?

When given a job to do, can I be depended upon to complete it to the best of my ability within the specified time?

Do people depend on me?

If not, why not?

If they do, how can I be of more help to them?

Should I encourage dependence?

23. Am I ready to learn?

Do I see a need for learning?

What have I learned this week?

Where did I learn it?

How can I use it?

Am I willing to change in any way necessary in order to put this learning into action?

Have I become stagnant in the learning process?

Do I feel I'm too old to learn?

Do I shy away from learning experiences because of my desire to remain a part of the authoritarian establishment rather than a part of the progressive thinking of the younger generation?

Do I feel I know everything I need to know in order to accomplish my task?

Do I feel that active learning will take away my stability and the comfortable feeling of knowing my subject or my people?

24. What motivates me?

Is it my love for Christ that led me to the mission field?

Is it a proper motivation?

Do I feel I have something to offer the world? If so, what?

Am I laboring to get recognition? Make a name for myself?

Do I feel compelled to be a missionary because the Word of God says I should be?

Did my family push me into it?

Would I rather do something else?

Do I need to be more deeply motivated?

Do I feel well qualified for the job I am doing?

Do I feel I must win the world for Christ?

Is my challenge as worthy and heartfelt today as it was the day I committed myself to Christ for full-time service?

25. How do I feel about unity?

What are my feelings about ecumenicity?

How do I support or attack it?

Have I thought it through?

How do I feel Christians can present a more united front?

How do I fit into the picture?

26. Am I outspoken?

    Shy?

    Afraid to speak up?

    Do I speak only when spoken to?

    Do I talk too much?

    Do I feel inferior? Superior?

    Do I always have to be heard?

    How good a listener am I?

    Do I think as much as I could and should?

    Am I happy to be laissez-faire, or do I want a piece of the action?

    Am I interested enough in my part in God's work to contribute all I possibly can to every situation in which I am involved?

27. Do I have special talents?

    What are they?

    How am I using them?

    Am I hiding them? Why?

    Am I proud of them?

    Do I volunteer them?

    Could I further develop them?

28. Do I feel comfortable within myself?

    Where could I improve?

    What makes me most uncomfortable?

    How can I overcome this?

29. Do I periodically evaluate myself, my work, my
    actions and reactions, my need for further
    learning or education, my attitudes, my
    behavior, my progress, my spiritual life?

    Am I going forward or backward?

    Quickly or slowly?

    Am I more mature now than when I first went to
    the mission field?

    Am I ready to put my heart into my deputation
    work?

    Do I have a message to share?

    Am I looking forward to sharing it?

30. Am I gracious and courteous?

    Do I find myself saying "thank you" more than
    ever before?

    Is my gratitude genuine?

    Do I take things and people for granted?

31. What is my attitude toward success?

    Do I allow myself the privilege of failing?

    Do I understand that success is relative?

    Do I demand more, or less of myself than of
    others?

    Is success my only goal?

    Have I failed the Lord when plans do not
    consummate as I feel they should?

    Who sets my standards for success?

    What does success mean to me?

32. Is my life characterized by humility?

    What does humility mean?

    Is it downgrading?

    Is it necessary for me to refuse to acknowledge all abilities and capabilities in order to maintain an aura of humility?

    Am I aware of being humble?

33. Have I set goals for myself?

    For my devotional life?

    For my family?

    For my work?

    For my co-workers?

    For the nationals?

    For my mission?

    For my term of service?

    For my furlough period?

    Have these been met?

    What difference does it make if they have?

    If not, why not?

34. Am I a good soldier of Jesus Christ?

    An ambassador without shame?

    A clean vessel for Him to use?

    An unchoked channel?

    A faithful steward?

An obedient love-slave?

Are there areas where improvements must be made?

35. Am I tired to death of being a "saint"?

Do I resent being a missionary? Lacking funds? Raising support? Being nice?

Am I sacrificing time and money on a cause which no longer appeals to me?

Am I ready to give it all up? Why?

What alternate plan do I have?

Will this plan work out better to my liking and keep me in the will of God?

Am I ready to embark on this new plan?

How do I know assuredly that this is God's perfect plan for my life?

B. MY WORK

1. Do I feel responsible to speak to every soul I meet concerning the claims of Jesus Christ?

How do I feel when I pass up an opportunity?

2. Have I felt my parish consisted of 40,000 souls?

Have I tried to reach the masses?

Have I spread myself and the message of the gospel too thin?

Would it be better to put my efforts into training just a few so that they could reach their own people?

Have my efforts been rewarded in salvation and/or growth?

If not, is there a reason for this?

3. Have I been diligent in language study?

   Have I taken every opportunity to learn to speak idiomatically and intelligently?

   Do I communicate understandably in my new tongue?

   Do I have the feeling people are laughing at my pronunciation, or my mistakes in grammar?

   Or is this secondary to the love I show and concern and care I have for those to whom I am speaking?

   Do I really care if I can speak the language well or not?

4. Have I been able to make decisions which have been required in controversial situations?

   Have I been able to counsel a new Christian who finds himself legally married to three wives?

   Do I find myself in full agreement that candidates for baptism must wait and be trained for a year or two before receiving baptism?

   Do I have the answer for those who fall into sin? For those seeking Scriptural solutions to daily problems? For the backslider?

   Am I seeking the answers to these questions and others like them if I have not determined in my own mind and heart what I believe to be correct?

5. Am I willing to allow nationals to be given positions of leadership in their churches?

   In my mission's work?

   Within my mission family?

   What is my attitude concerning their financial support?

6. Have I shared my goals for the work with others on my station?

   Have we sought to share goals and work to see that they are met?

   Have I felt my goals must be met at the expense of anyone or anything?

   Have they been attained?

   Where have they taken us?

   Were they good goals? Attainable?

7. Have I experimented with new methods?

   Have I used audio-visual tools?

   In my specialized work, have I been willing to teach others? Missionaries? Nationals?

   Did it prove to be helpful?

   Have I been reticent about sharing my hard-earned knowledges and skills with others?

8. Have I withheld anything from my national brethren to assure my presence with them for an unlimited time?

   Do I feel it is better if the work remains in the hands of the missionaries?

   How much am I preparing the nationals for my work in the event I should have to leave?

   Do I trust them with responsibility? Authority? Finances?

9. Have I looked for opportunities to expand my ministry and the effectiveness of it?

   Or have I been content to do only what was demanded of me?

   What does the second mile involve?

10. Have I been willing to be moved from my station?

    Am I flexible?

    If word arrives during my furlough that I will be assigned to a different work or area, what will be my reaction?

    Will it depend upon what work and what area?

    Am I willing for some changes, but not others?

    Is my reaction based upon fear? Dislike for a certain situation? Co-workers? Rumors?

11. Am I willing to take a leadership position when requested, even though I do not feel prepared for it?

    Am I willing to play a lesser role when I feel I should be granted a place of authority?

12. How does my work advance the cause of Christ?

    How does it fit into the entire scope of my mission's work?

    Can I cooperate with other missions in the area?

    Do I really feel it is *my* work?

13. As a wife, how much time should I spend in the work?

    Should I give 100% of my time to my family?

    How can I best make my children happy in our adopted country?

    How do I feel about my children having to be separated from us for long periods of time while they are in school?

    How much time do I spend worrying that they will pick up a disease, learn things they shouldn't from national children, or become too nationalized?

Should I take my children with me when I do village visitation?

Should I hire a woman to care for the children in our home so I can continue my missionary responsibilities?

Am I jealous of my husband's work?

How do I feel about the fact he has to go away for several days or weeks on mission business?

14. Is it wrong to take days off from my missionary work?

Do I feel an 8-hour day should be the rule for missionaries?

Is my time for study and research of benefit?

Should I do more of it?

Do I feel others think I am wasting time?

15. Are there items of equipment which I need to obtain during furlough which will facilitate the work when I return to the field?

16. Is my work satisfying to me?

How could it be made more so?

Do I feel I'm doing a good job?

Do I need more help?

Are nationals actively involved in the ministry?

Is this to my liking?

Do I respect them? Resent them?

Do I feel stymied because of lack of finances for the work?

Am I happy doing itinerant work, or would I prefer

to stay in one place?

What is best for me, the work, the mission?

17. How do I feel about the country where I serve?

    Does their philosophical approach irritate me?

    Do I detest reporting every move I make to the local police?

    Am I aware of every move I make because I know the CIA or other authorities are closely watching me?

    Am I offended by this?

    Do I cheat a little now and then on the restrictions laid down for me by my host government?

    Do I feel guilty about this?

18. Do I evaluate the work at definite intervals?

    Who helps me with this?

    Do I ever ask for help?

    From whom?

    If we're not reaching our objectives, am I willing to change my approach?

    Or do I merely delay the reaching of the goal?

    Do I set new goals?

    Are these goals made known?

    Are they realistic?

19. How do I feel when nationalism overpowers Christianity in the lives of national believers?

    Am I discouraged? Do I try to make them less nationalized? More Christian?

20. Do I try to make the national church a miniature of the church in my homeland?

    Do I insist on western patterns of culture for all men everywhere?

    How do I feel about drinking from a common communion cup?

    Do I feel illiterates can make a contribution to the local church?

21. Do I preach only salvation, neglecting spiritual food for young Christians?

    Am I interested in a literacy program so these people can come to read the Word of God for themselves?

    Is a Bible School available in my field?

    If not, should we start one?

    What is my personal feeling concerning nationals being sent to my homeland for Bible or technical training?

C. MY INTER-PERSONAL RELATIONSHIPS

    1. Am I openly antagonistic?

       Am I set in my ways?

       Am I open to the opinions of others?

       Do I give a strong reaction before hearing out the other fellow?

    2. Am I careful in my behavior?

       Do I consider what effect my actions and attitudes will have on others? Missionaries? Nationals?

       Am I crushed when others behave in a way which dishonors the Savior?

Do I, in love, speak to my brother or sister, admonishing? Scolding?

Do I have a different set of standards for the missionary and the national?

3. Do I honestly feel that the Christian nationals with whom I work are on a par with me?

Do I condemn their lack of formal education, their need for money and material things, their discipline of their children (or lack of it), their ways of witnessing?

Do I feel they are somewhat inferior to me in intelligence?

Do I look down on them?

Do I look up to them?

Does the color of their skin have any bearing on my feelings?

Is their way of doing things inferior to mine?

Do they have customs I would like to emulate?

Do I envy them?

Do I try to understand them?

Do I feel they owe me respect?

Do I feel I should be in charge and they should remain subservient to me?

Would I be willing to work under their direction?

4. How understanding am I?

How insistent am I?

Do I run away from situations I don't understand?

Do I condemn quickly?

Do I look further into those things which I do
not understand, or which I feel I may have
misinterpreted or misunderstood?

Even when something seems legally, morally,
physically or spiritually wrong, do I attempt
to find the true motives for the action?

5. Am I able to communicate with my fellow-workers?
Even when I'm upset?

Am I honest in my communications?

Am I able to look someone in the eye and admit
I disagree with him?

Do words become heated in discussions?

Am I discerning?

Do I listen?

Am I patient?

Do I feel things inside that I refuse to express?

Does this cause hostility to unleash itself, or
build up within me?

When it does, how does it affect my communication?

6. Am I, as a single person, jealous of privileges
given to married couples? (Time away from
the station with children, fellowship and
sharing with other married couples, family
times, etc.).

Do I feel that I, as a single missionary, am
expected to be more flexible than they? Be
sent from one place to another without being
asked? Made to babysit for children of senior
missionaries?

Am I certain my senior missionary sees no need
for single girls, finds them immature, weepy,
unstable, and unfit for their job assignment?

Does my senior missionary *really* feel that way, or could I be wrong?

Have I felt like an outsider on the station?

Have I been wife- or husband-seeking?

Has my conduct with the nationals always been above and beyond reproach?

Am I jealous of my married co-workers?

Do I have a secret love? A national? A married colleague?

What is my conviction concerning marriage to a national?

7. Am I, as a married missionary, careful not to look down on single folks as though there were something lacking in them?

Do I try to include them occasionally in family plans?

Do I allow them to fellowship with one another?

Do I expect more work of a better quality from them than I do from married folks?

Do I feel they should be free for any task at anytime of the day or night?

Do I feel that single folks cause many problems on the field because of their insecurity, loneliness, jealousy, shyness or instability?

How have I tried to help the situation?

Have I been too critical?

Have I tried to understand and to put myself in their situation?

Have I secretly condemned them for their unmarried state? Envied them?

8. Do I feel a missionary should work an 8-hour day, 5-day week?

   Do I rebel at interruptions during my "non-working hours"?

   Do I feel a missionary should work 24-hours a day, 7 days a week?

   Do I bear a grudge against a co-worker who feels differently than I do concerning the work week?

   Do I consider my co-workers before taking time away from my station?

   Do I plan my vacation in cooperation with others who must bear the burden of the work during my absence?

   Do I contrive and make excuses for being away from my station as often as possible?

9. Are there co-workers with whom I cannot get along?

   What are the basic problems?

   What have I done to help the situation?

   To hinder it?

   Am I willing for a reconciliation or working agreement?

   Or do I want to hang on to my grievance(s)?

   Are our personality conflicts beyond the grace of God?

   Is the blame as much mine as it is my co-worker's?

10. Have I shown favoritism to certain nationals?

    Is this wrong?

Has it produced hard feelings?

Do I prefer to ignore nationals if it is a
  choice of fellowship with them or with friends
  from the homeland?

Do I feel at home with nationals?

Can I share with them? Pray with them?

11. Am I interested in the needs of others?

  Do I try to give comfort, counsel and consolation
    when it is needed or requested?

  Do I enter into the joys and sorrows of others?

  Do I try to become involved, or am I content to
    remain on the sidelines?

12. Do I respect the training and experience of
    younger missionaries?

  Do I feel they have something to offer me and
    the work?

  Or do I feel they should be seen and not heard
    for at least the first term of service?

  Do I welcome new folks to the field?

  Do I try to remember some of the adjustments
    I had to face, and then seek to understand how
    the new folks feel and what they are facing?

  Do I endeavor to help as much as possible in
    this adjustment?

  Or do I let them grope for themselves as I was
    made to do?

13. Do I respect the authority and knowledge of my
    senior missionaries?

  Do I automatically label them "out-dated"?

Do I accept younger missionaries and weigh and utilize their opinions and contributions?

Do I try to force my opinions on others?

Do I openly rebel when things don't go my way?

Do I downgrade the mission, its workers, and its ministry by refusing to work in harmony with my fellow-workers?

Do I fellowship only with those in my own age group?

Do I feel unaccepted by mission leaders?

14. Do I respect the confidences of others?

Do I offer fellowship in prayer?

Do I offer my services as freely to my fellow-missionaries as to the nationals?

15. Do my children know I love them?

Is there any cause for them to feel they are only third or fourth place in my heart?

Do I run to the aid of others when they need me, but insist by attitude and action that my own children should handle their problems with little or no help from me?

Do I allow my children any freedom of decision?

Or is their life a list of do's and don'ts laid down by me?

Have I made them come to understand why we are missionaries?

Do they have any share in the work?

Do they know they are wanted and needed?

Do I openly criticize my work, the workers, and the mission in front of my children?

Do I help them to have a happy relationship with national children, or do I make them feel they are superior and should, therefore, not associate with nationals?

Do my children seek counsel from me or do they go to others for help?

Is our home as free of tension as is possible?

Are there any double standards in my code of morality?

Do my children love me? Respect me?

Are they glad I'm a missionary? Am I?

Do they want to pursue Christian training and work?

Are they allowed to be less than perfect?

Is my discipline of them suitable and carried out in love?

Are they allowed a life of their own when they come of age?

16. When my fellow-workers do not have as much as I do, am I willing to share with them?

Do I expect to be repaid?

Do I do it out of duty, or concern?

17. Am I willing to take an active part in mission prayer meetings?

Have I been interested in inter-mission activities?

Can I be counted upon to give a hand if needed for a special ministry in my area?

If a co-worker is sick, on vacation, or on furlough, am I willing to fulfill his obligations so that the work will continue to move forward?

Or would I delight to see it collapse?

Perhaps these questions will help in your evaluation of your field experience as well as providing goals toward which you can expect to move during your furlough period and upon your return to the field.

Be strictly honest in your answers. No one else needs to know those answers, but they should help you to become a better person and a more effective missionary. It may even help you to come to know yourself.

May God bless you as you seek to grow in grace and continue to follow the Lord to the ends of the earth.

8

Living Within Your Budget

Your first trip to a store in the homeland will leave you in a state of shock, whether you are buying clothing, food, children's toys, a car, or postage stamps. Were things this expensive two, three or four years ago? No, of course not. But they really haven't increased in price as much as they appear to you. The simple fact of the matter is that the entire economic structure has altered since your last visit home.

Even if you are returning from a country whose economy is on more of a par with the homeland, you will still feel prices are outrageously high. It used to be possible to at least get good hamburger rather inexpensively. But no longer. And unless you want to live on potatoes, beans and rice, the food bill for your family will seem all out of proportion. And with the price of food in restaurants, there will be few meals out in the days ahead. (All of this will, of course, make you appreciate, more than ever, the hospitality given to you in the homes of others).

It *will* be difficult to live within your limited budget in the homeland, but you will learn to do it just as other families do. The diet will not often include sirloin steaks or legs of lamb. But it is possible to shop for and purchase nourishing food. Watch for sales at the local food stores. Also try, as much

as possible, to buy store name brands of tins and jars
of food rather than national name brands. The quantity
and quality of the food is usually excellent, but the
cost is lower. Less expensive cuts of meat can be
cooked in such a way that they are tender, tasty, and
appetizing. Exotic and specialty foods may not get to
your table, but good, wholesome, nourishing food will.
If you are fortunate enough to own a freezer, or have
access to one, it is possible to get some very good
prices on frozen products. Frozen fruits and vegetables
are often on sale. Be sure to buy the "family-size"
packages which run far less per pound than the smaller
packets. Vegetables packed in pouches with butter or
cheese sauces are far more expensive than those which
are frozen by themselves. Many areas have "day-old"
bakery outlets where bread and pastries can be purchased very inexpensively. During the course of a
year of furlough, enough money could be saved by buying
food this way to more than pay for a freezer, depending
upon the size of your family.

In meal planning, it is good to have only one large
meal per day. You will not be able to afford bacon for
breakfast every day. Eggs and bulk cereal will be your
mainstay for breakfast. Milk purchased by the gallon
is less expensive than by the quart. Bulk cheese is
less expensive than fancy wedges. Fruit and vegetables
can be purchased from farm markets during the season.
In some areas, you have opportunity to pick your own
tomatoes, cucumbers, beans, peppers, oranges, grape-
fruit, strawberries or blueberries, paying very little
per quart or bag. Canning your own fruits and vegetables
can save money.

A woman who can make clothes for her family is most
fortunate. The cost of a sewing machine will be repaid
after she makes two or three dresses for herself! Or
she may wish to rent a machine during furlough. With
the many cloth outlets available with very attractive
prices for fine materials, clothing can be made inexpensively. Buying a wardrobe at regular retail prices
can be devastating to the pocketbook.

There are many discount houses, and stores that
through quantity buying or manufacture, are able to offer
much better prices than independent stores can offer.

Always look for quality in these stores. If you know
values, you will be able to do very well. But if you
can only compare prices, and you decide on an item just
because it is less expensive than advertised somewhere
else, you may discover that with very little effort
your seams are splitting, your handle is loose or your
wheels are coming off!

When looking for transportation for your furlough
time, try not to buy the first used car offered to you
inexpensively from the lot. You will probably put
many thousands of miles on it, and you will do well to
get the best car you can afford. Some missionaries are
fortunate enough to have friends who loan or buy them a
car for furlough use. Others must bear this expense
themselves. Some are able to obtain a good used car
from a missionary just returning to the field from
furlough. Others may feel they will not bother to buy
a car for the three months of furlough, if they have
chosen the short furlough option.

If you do think of getting transportation, however,
there are many things which must be taken into consideration: The size of the family, the size of the car,
the make, the cost, the model, the upkeep, a new compact
or a used medium size, a car, van or station wagon,
6-cylinder or 8-cylinder, automatic, semi-automatic or
stick shift, how much you plan to travel, resale value,
etc.

If you are a single girl, and know nothing about
automobiles, either buy from someone you know and
trust, or take a friend with you who knows what should
be under the hood. Remember that even a used-car guaran-
tee will do little good if you have a breakdown in the
Arizona desert.

If housing is not provided for you, you may have to
add funds from your personal support to stretch your
housing allowance to meet your needs. This means even
less money available for food and clothing.

Even though it may be difficult to make your dollars
purchase all that is needed, you will have many opportunities to see God provide for you in many ways.

Missionaries on furlough have not yet had to beg bread. Meals, clothing, housing needs, equipment and travel funds will be provided from unexpected sources. Trust Him for it and He will prove once again that "Faithful is He that calleth you who also will do it." (I Thess. 5:24).

9

Speaking Engagements

There are two kinds of missionaries:

1. Those who thoroughly enjoy deputation work, and

2. Those who thoroughly dislike it.

In the majority of situations, it matters little how the missionary feels about this ministry, for it is expected of him, and therefore it must be done - even the pilot who stutters and the doctor who is quiet and uncommunicative. Of course an alternative could be to schedule a full course of schooling for the entire length of furlough. Your wife could take care of the speaking. Marriage does have certain such benefits! But what of the shy, single bookkeeper? The mechanic who has kept the mission vehicles operating and saved the missionaries thousands of dollars who may be a dud on the market when it comes to speaking in public? Some folks do very well in small groups, chatting over a cup of coffee, or showing slides with a taped narration in a darkened room. But enlarge the group, take away the stimulant, and turn on the lights, and the missionary becomes panic-stricken and speechless.

Among the missionaries who enjoy deputation work, we have three main types:

1. Those who say so little and use such vague
descriptions that the minds of their listeners
are left totally or partially blank.

2. Those who have a well-prepared message or
presentation which has great appeal to
the group.

3. Those who feel this is their hour to shine
in eloquence, and who, therefore, drone on
and on and on - usually leaving their hearers
behind after the first 20 minutes.

Let's face it. When did you last sit still and completely absorbed in a long-winded or uninteresting speaker?

As a missionary, you are a very fortunate person.
You have something worthwhile to say, you will usually
have a sympathetic audience, you will actually have an
opportunity to challenge people to share in missions by
involvement, you have travelled, you have lived with
people about whom your audience knows very little, you
have had experiences which they will never face, you have
seen problems arise and be solved in unique ways, you
have committed your life to Jesus Christ for service in
a situation about which your hearers know little or
nothing. But you're not a speaker? Do you mean you
never converse or communicate with anyone at any time?

Speaking to a group of people, whether many or few,
known or unknown, can be a terrifying experience to shy
people whose self-image and/or ego strength are less
than needed for this type of work. But remember, your
audience is made up of individuals just like you. You
are sharing with each one in the group your enthusiasm
about your work. Among supporting churches, you are
sharing *their* work with them, for they have had a real
part in your service by gifts and prayers and personal
concern.

Your knees and hands may be shaking, but your
listeners will never notice. They aren't against you!
They're for you all the way. They're interested or they
wouldn't have come. They're interested in you as a
person as well as in what you have to share with them.

What do they want to hear? This should not be
difficult to decide. When you hear a speaker, what do
YOU want to know? What type of presentation do YOU
prefer? What appeals to you? What turns you off?
Only by speaking in terms of what is relevant and exciting to you can you hope to capture the attention
of those to whom you will speak.

Perhaps you feel that *what* you say is the important
part of speaking. Or perhaps you fear that *how* you say
it is most essential. The final answer will probably
involve both of these elements by the effective organization of your thoughts. It is very important that you
strive to point to one theme in what you say in each
meeting. Don't scatter ideas like buckshot. This type
of presentation usually develops when the speaker is
not well prepared. The less prepared a person is in
anything he undertakes, the less poise he will have and
the less impression he will make. An outline of what
you are going to say is imperative. You may even wish
to share this with your listeners so they can be prepared to follow you. Make your outline simple, but
inviting. Don't tell everything you know by means of
your outline. It has been aptly stated that to produce
the best retention of material, it is best to *tell people
what you're going to tell them, tell them, and tell them
what you've told them!* It is also true that unless you
are an exceptionally capable speaker, lecture-type
speaking cannot hold the attention of your listeners for
more than 20 minutes. Thus you may wish to use several
methods of presentation, breaking off the lecture and
showing slides or a movie, or providing for questions
and answers.

Your meetings will be mainly of an informal nature.
Conversational type speaking will be the order of the
day. Although some people say you should speak "just
above the heads" of your listeners, others say to pick
out a friendly face and speak to it. The truth of the
matter is, however, that you must speak in order to
reach every individual present, whether you have an
audience of 5 or 500.

Part of the attention you receive will be derived
from your own involvement in your subject. If you're
excited about it and have a desire to share it with

others, your enthusiasm will catch on. Try not to scream at your listeners. Don't mumble. Speak as friend to friend. Don't be overdramatic. Try not to adjust your glasses, pull your ear, scratch your nose, or jingle the change in your pocket continually.

In summary, then, be sure to plan well what you are going to say and how you are going to say it; tell your audience what you feel will be most interesting to them; be honest; be yourself; if stories are used to illustrate your lecture, make them short and meaningful (some speakers give the life stories of 3 converts, using 30 minutes to do so, and lose their hearers after the first 5 minutes); be sure your illustrations do not overpower what you are trying to say, but rather enhance your message by stressing the main points; your audience is friendly and appreciative – try not to be afraid of them; maintain rapport will *all* your listeners. Relax as much as possible and try to enjoy your presentation as much as you hope your listeners will. If you feel you have nothing to say, it might be good to ask yourself some questions as to why you feel that way. Perhaps in such a case your furlough should be spent finding challenge for your own life rather than attempting to challenge others.

Deputation can be a fun thing. Entered into whole-heartedly, it can be rewarding in many ways. The fellowship of those who are interested in you and your work can be a sustaining force in your life.

If you are a married couple, and both are present at a service, perhaps the speaking time can be shared; or one can speak, the other show slides; or one can present in the church while the other is speaking to the young people or Sunday School group. If your children are with you, you may want them to participate in the meetings, or they may be asked to speak or sing, or be introduced. Never force them into a situation that will embarrass them. But if they *want* to be included, don't exclude them.

In your speaking, remember the time limits extended to you. Never go over your time, even when you have been cut back at the last moment from 15 minutes to 2. Return invitations are sometimes not given to those whose "tongue runs completely".

When speaking to a group, avoid controversial
issues. There are doctrinal beliefs which are not
tolerated in some groups; certain men cannot be mentioned in some churches; certain social issues cannot
be upheld or condemned; never take sides in church
disputes; do not degrade people, denominations, missions
or yourself.

But don't concern yourself unduly with the negatives.
The natural, honest, pleasant speaker will avoid un-
pleasant subjects and will willingly share his field,
his work, his people, his hopes, his experiences with
those who have come to listen.

Because of the many speakers who pass through a
church each year, your presentation should be unique.
A mediocre meeting will not be a lasting remembrance
unless your people already know you and are involved in
your ministry. (Even then, you must give it your utmost).

Be sure to give a balanced view of your work and your
field. There was a time when it seemed missionaries
felt compelled to tell only the bright side of missions.
Today your congregation will expect reality. A completely optimistic or pessimistic report will leave
many questions unanswered in the minds of your hearers.
Young people will not be challenged nearly so much by
hearing that your field and work is utopian as they will
if you tell it like it is, with its aspects of joy and
sorrow, pleasure and disappointment.

Don't apologize for what you have to say. No
matter how insecure you feel as a speaker, be positive
in what you say. Speak about that in which you are
most comfortable and knowledgeable. Picture yourself
as a listener rather than a speaker. Especially at
missionary conferences, where you have opportunity to
hear other speakers, pick out those who appeal to you.
What made you listen attentively to them? What was
their approach? Usually you will find that the enthusiasm of the speaker in what he is saying far sur-
passes the words he says in gaining the enthusiastic
response of his hearers. If your work does not thrill
you, you will never be able to interest others. How

sad it is when a missionary comes home after four years on the field and says "I really have nothing to say."

Keep in mind that human interest is of utmost importance in your speaking. An engineer will be thrilled about his amps, ohms and watts. A pilot will be enthused about his rudder, guages and propellers. A secretary will be ear deep in her typing, transcribing and telephoning. A photographer will be involved with film speeds, lenses and composition. But when these folks come back to the homeland, their audiences will be interested in what happened to *people* because of their use of these components of their daily work.

Although you should involve the emotions of your listeners as well as their minds, it is unfair to play upon the sympathies of congregations. It is not the best way to gain *lasting* support.

When you are asked to speak at any service, be selective in what you present. It is impossible to present a full picture of you, your mission, your field and your work. Dwell on one aspect and deal with it adequately. Decide what you want your listeners to remember more than anything else. Aim for that one focal point. This does not mean that you cannot give background material, but you must be sure to direct your hearers to something they will remember.

If you are in a church for a conference with other speakers, or a week of meetings by yourself, you may find some difficulty in presenting your field to various groups and the same group again and again. Each service should build upon that which you have told before, not a repetition of what you have stated previously. Sometimes your host church will outline what they would like to hear. But often it will be up to you to outline your meetings. Do it carefully after much prayer and preparation.

Be sure to find out before you attend a meeting whether they expect a strictly missionary presentation, a Bible study on the theme of missions, or just a Bible study. This can save a lot of grief.

Some of you will have your personal support pledged.

This should not keep you from being prepared to speak
and represent your Board. And don't be afraid to be as
enthusiastic about a general presentation for your
mission as you are about gaining your own support.

Others will be fully supported through their Board
and will be asked to go on tour with 2 or 3 missionaries
from other fields within their mission's scope of
responsibility, appearing primarily at missionary conventions. Although you will present your own work,
you will also need to be prepared to give your testimony,
to challenge your audiences from the Word of God concerning their response to missions, and to uphold your
Mission Board and gain support for it. But since you
will travel widely, it will be possible to work out
a basic outline of what you wish to present during a
week of meetings. When churches are separated by long
distances, you will be able to use your messages many
times. In doing so, however, be sure that they are,
at all times, as fresh and inspiring the tenth time as
they are the first. When *you* begin to tire of a certain
presentation, change it. Otherwise your boredom will
be transferred to your hearers.

Speaking in deputation meetings is a great privilege.
It is one of the important reasons for a furlough. It
is the means by which others are encouraged to participate in the greatest work in the world - missions.

May God bless you as you seek to honor and glorify
Him in each of your meetings and may He encourage you
with a positive response from those to whom you speak.

10

Using Slides And
Movies In Your Meetings

Missionaries usually take movies, slides or pictures during their term on the field. They may be taken with little prior experience in the art of picture-taking. They have no form or design. They are not the pictures you now wish you had taken, and you regret that you did not have a plan and goal, but merely shot here and there at this and that. You also wish you had taken more pictures upon your arrival on the field when everything engulfed you because it was new and different. After a while, everything was so commonplace that it did not seem necessary to "shoot" it. But whatever you've captured on celluloid, avoid the following in your meetings:

1. You show a picture of your national church group - 75 individuals. You then proceed to tell the life story of the 7th man from the left in the next to last row. To make matters worse, the picture was taken from a distance of 50 feet because you wanted to get the entire church building in the background. And unbelievably, after 5 minutes on Raphael's life story, you tell the conversion history of two others in the group. (You not only lose your audience, but you can burn up your film by keeping it in front of a 500-watt bulb for ten minutes)!

2. You didn't have your slides set up before the
   meeting. Therefore in your rush to put them
   in the tray, four get in upside down and two
   go in sideways. This can take away from the
   effectiveness of what you are trying to present!

3. There is one slide in the midst of the rest
   which is a double exposure (or overexposed,
   or underexposed). You explain that this is the
   only picture you were able to obtain of this
   individual or thing, and ask forgiveness for
   it not being a better shot. It's so poor that
   it would have been far better to leave it out.

4. You weren't really used to setting your new
   camera accurately. The shots are just a bit
   fuzzy or blurry. The projectionist tries
   frantically to bring the scenes into sharpest
   focus, going from blur to blur. The congregation decides, individually and collectively,
   that they really must make that appointment
   with the eye doctor(especially if they're
   over 40), and you go merrily on your way describing the pictures as though they had been
   taken by a professional photographer!

5. You describe your pictures, but don't speak
   loudly enough for people to hear.

6. You have a tape recording to be played to
   describe your pictures. So people will be
   sure to hear, you place the machine in front
   of a microphone. The quality of the recording
   and its closeness to the mike make the words
   unintelligible, and its shrillness and loudness
   give everyone a headache.

7. You insist on operating the projector yourself.
   It's a machine with which you are not familiar.
   The slides jam, or the 16mm film rolls on the
   floor instead of on the take-up reel. The lights
   are on and off so many times that it entirely
   disrupts any continuity that may have been
   intended.

8. You were able to get some really good shots in the Mission Hospital operating room - close-ups of amputations, bleeding gunshot wounds, weeping sores; you were also fortunate enough to visit a leprosarium where you took close-up views of men and women minus noses, fingers, toes, and other parts of the anatomy. These are best shown, of course, at Medical Conventions. In public meetings, especially with women and children present, either don't show such pictures, or be sure to provide plenty of smelling salts and basins.

9. Naked natives are not usually best shown on wide screen in mixed audiences. You may be working amongst people who do not wear clothes. To you the scenes are natural, typical and true to life. But to pastors of churches, they may not be the type of films they want shown, and it is up to them to decide where, how and when such pictures should be used. Never show nakedness on the screen without prior approval.

10. Don't show more than 80 slides in a meeting unless many shots are shown rapidly as different angles of the same person or thing or theme. Many times, 40 slides will be sufficient, but it depends upon how much you describe each view and the length of time allotted to you.

11. If you show slides and then speak concerning your field and its work, don't merely repeat what you said during the slide presentation. Build and elaborate on it.

12. Don't depend entirely upon your slides or movies to present your work. YOU are more important to your audience than your visual presentation.

In spite of all the don'ts we've mentioned, there are some more positive things to remember for you presentation:

1. Limit your presentation to the time designated for it.

2. Have some order to your slides or film so that
    they focus on a given theme. You may want to
    have several slide sets or films available,
    depending upon the emphasis you seek to stress.

3. Explain the scenes, so they will be meaningful
    to those who watch.

4. Move the program along, spending no more than
    15 or 20 seconds on each slide. In rare
    instances you may wish to spend as long as a
    minute - but please, no longer. Also, 10 seconds
    is the minimal time for a slide to be viewed
    properly.

5. Show your best slides, fewer groups and more
    close-ups, scenery to set the climate, and then
    an emphasis upon your ministry.

6. Take into account the type of group to whom
    you are speaking. Gear your descriptions to
    them.

7. Consider the size of your group as to how
    loudly you should speak, how far the projector
    should be from the screen, how close the tape
    recorder should be to the microphone. Unless
    people can see and hear, the meeting is so much
    wasted time.

8. Try to show your work as thoroughly as possible
    by means of pictures. Your listeners remember
    far more of what they see than of what they
    hear.

9. Use slides or films with which you are familiar.

10. When you are using a projectionist, arrange
    beforehand what signal you will use when it is
    time to move on. It is very disruptive to have
    to say after each scene, "The next slide, please."

As you speak from time to time, you will be making
mental notes as to pictures you will obtain upon your
return to the field. You may even prepare several slide-
tape series for next furlough if you didn't do so for
this one.

Some missionaries hold their finger across the lens, shake the camera, or become discouraged with mechanical gadgets. These are they who don't take a camera with them to the field. As a last desperate effort, they borrow slides from friends and may not be sure what they have obtained. Or perhaps they have borrowed a series from the Mission Office. Unfortunately, a picture-less secretary ends up with a series on the engineering accomplishments of the mission, about which she knows little or nothing. (Isn't it amazing how cloistered we can become in our own ministry with little or no understanding of what our fellow-missionaries are accomplishing)? As far as effectiveness is concerned, it would be far better to admit to no pictures!

We've spoken of the negatives, and it would not be fair to pass by without congratulating those many missionaries who have realized that up-to-date pictures from the field are important and necessary, those who have taken excellent pictures with inexpensive cameras, have put together a good display of photographic material, and are using it as a means of a vivid, graphic, detailed analysis of their country and their work. They have included pictures of themselves on the job; they have thrown away every poor shot; they have planned their slide or film presentation as carefully - perhaps more so - than any message they will give during furlough. They find their presentations are effective, stimulating, descriptive, thought-provoking, informative, and worth all the time and effort put into them.

Your mission may have excellent, professionally filmed, 16mm sound color movies available for your use. Keep these in mind for missionary conferences. It is not ideal, however, to use your Mission's film on Japan if you are working in Zambia, no matter how good the film is. People are interested primarily in YOU and YOUR work unless you have been specifically asked to represent your mission in a general way. The latter is usually left up to the Deputation Secretary or Regional Representatives. If the film happens to depict your own field, use it freely, for it should be well-planned and better organized than your own unprofessional movies which are pieced together.

In using either slides or movies, it is possible to create clever titles without too much difficulty. If filming movie titles, be sure to take enough footage to allow the audience to read it unhurriedly.

It should be kept in mind that slides and films are not an end in themselves. They must be used with care as an adjunct to the speaker, not in place of him. They are an educational tool - not a movie show. Movies, if well taken, put together and presented will give a better picture of actual living scenes since they show motion, cover a large range of subject matter, cover progress and development, bridge time and space, and better put the viewer into the scene.

Pictures tend to clarify some of the false impressions people get when listening to a speaker. When the word "desert" is mentioned, minds think of barren sands spread under a hot sun. Pictures show that a "desert" can have trees, shrubs, grass, canals, villages, railroads, airports, animals and people. One hears the word "equator" and assumes the worker lives in a hot, wet jungle where temperatures are unbearably warm. Pictures show the equator can be 10,000 feet above sea level with snow-capped volcanoes, fertile valleys, and cold days and nights. And we could go on with such analogies. "A picture is worth a thousand words." But be sure it is a *good* picture.

To make slides or a film (which you would narrate) more interesting, involve your audience. Before the showing, toss out several questions which can be answered by the visual aid (e.g. name the animals pictured, what is the name of the school, where is the station located, in what type of homes do the people live, how many teachers do you have in the school, etc.). These questions will be answered in the brief showing of your pictures (not more than 5 minutes and no more than 10 seconds per slide). Then the service will take on an informal pattern, thus alleviating the need for lecturing. The more people you can involve, the more interested they will become. After your specific questions have been answered, allow others to ask questions. To close the meeting, show the same pictures, explaining them, thus making a deeper impression upon the minds of those who watch. This is particularly effective with children and young people.

One further word is necessary. You may be prepared to show an excellent film or series of slides. You have proven by its use in scores of services that it is effective. But do prepare for an alternate program which will cover the same amount of time. For the electricity can go off unexpectedly; your projector can blow its last bulb as you turn it on; you may be given less time in the program at the last minute and you will not be able to show your slides or film (especially if you have a tape recorded message or description); you may drop your slides and get them out of order; or the projector which was promised for your use never arrives. As always, *"be prepared to preach, pray, die, or get married at a moment's notice"* and go on with your presentation - minus visuals - as though you had planned it that way. Please don't apologize in every other sentence concerning this dire turn of events. Most of all, don't panic. Everyone will live through the experience!

11

Use Of Other Audio-Visual Aids

Often when we think of audio-visual aids for meetings, we think only of 2 x 2 slides and 8mm or 16mm movies. But there are many aids which are just as effective in presenting your missionary ministry to all age and ability groups. Not every group responds to audio-visual stimuli in the same way, so it is necessary to use a variety of means and methods. Films of every kind have been overworked. Much of their glamor has been long since lost through the fact that people have come to expect missionaries to use slides or a film if he isn't going to lecture.

But let's look at a variety of other tools which can be utilized by the missionary on furlough:

1. Flat pictures. These can be obtained on the field from shops, calendars, newspapers, books, advertising, etc. and made into notebooks, mounted on heavy paper or poster board, titled, and used in small groups, or be left on the display table for private perusing. They can also be used as a backdrop for a display or literature table, or projected on a screen by means of an opaque projector. Pictures should be colorful, chosen with care, and tell a definite story just as a film or slide series.

2. Photographs. These should be no smaller than 8" x 10". They can be used in the same way as

flat pictures. They are especially effective
in Sunday School classes, home presentations
and individual contacts. Be sure that the
pictures are properly exposed and developed,
with good contrast, depth of field and clear
detail. They must tell a story to be effective.
Pictures showing unique scenes, or contrasts,
are good. It is possible to have a series of
photographs showing close-ups of various types
of people among whom you work.

3. Overhead projectors are an excellent means of
showing distinctive materials to any-sized
audience. Preparation of materials can be
readily accomplished. Transparencies made can
be used time and again. Any type of graph,
chart, illustration, etc. can be marked on
acetate. Colored pictures and other materials
can be "lifted" and used effectively. This
projector can be used in an undarkened room
which is an advantage for daytime showing.

4. Opaque projectors can transfer to a screen
any material you may wish to show a group.
Material from books, clippings, maps, post
cards, magazines - even objects - can be projected. This takes a fully darkened room, so
keep this in mind.

5. Filmstrips. These are inexpensively made by
most reputable photographic companies. They
can use slides which you have taken or clips
from your movies. They are a cross between
slides and movies and can be used with a taped
or "in-person" narration.

6. Graphs. For small groups, statistical material
can be well presented by means of flat drawings employing means to visualize data. For
comparisons, analyses, or interpretation, graphs
are exceptionally good. There are several
kinds of graphs to tell your story quickly and
easily:

    a. Bar graphs can suitably show comparative
    religions, population, Christian community,
    etc.

    b. Circle graphs show how a whole is divided into parts and can be used to tell what percentage of missionaries are in various professional roles, number of national to missionary worker ratio, division of your total support figure into its proper categories (personal support, housing, transportation, health care, retirement, etc.), divisions of peoples among whom you labor (various tribes, groups, whites, blacks, etc.).

    c. Line graphs can plot the conclusion of trends such as how soon nationals may take over positions now occupied by missionaries, increased funds needed to complete certain projects, number of trained nationals available for the future expansion of the work, etc.

7.   Charts. These help your interested friends and supporters to understand better the task you and your Board are undertaking. There are many kinds of charts such as *flow charts* (to show sequence and relationship), *stream charts* (how several events converge, thus forming one large event, e.g. showing why a Bible School became a necessity), *tree charts* (reversing the stream chart, thus beginning with one large event and showing the small events of which it consists), *process charts* (showing how something is made, e.g., the conversion of an unbeliever), *map charts* (dots or symbols indicating your Mission's stations in a given country or national churches in your area). Charts cannot be used in large crowds, require time and skill in preparation, but can highlight key points, increase interest and attract attention. It is even possible to lightly pencil your chart and then draw it in front of your audience with a black marker pen. There are many varieties of charts including flip charts, slip charts, poster charts and pinboard charts.

8.   Posters. Use a single idea and utilize symbolism and slogans. Good for emphasizing what you want

from your hearers, e.g., go, give, pray, write, prepare, etc.

9. Diagrams and Sketches. You may wish to show how your hospital is laid out, what your people look like, types of clothing worn, where your radio antennae are located, and areas which you are reaching.

10. Maps and Globes. These are helpful in establishing relative positions and sizes. They pinpoint your area of responsibility. They can show physical features by color. Outline maps may be used so you can mark on them that which is pertinent in a given meeting. Wall maps are very acceptable, but arrange a place for them to be hung, or people to hold them at the time of your presentation.

11. Chalkboards. Any information, drawings, cartoons, or graphic material can be easily placed on a slate with chalk. Be sure to print large and legibly. Use various colored chalk to produce a more professional-looking effect.

12. Phonographs and Tape Recorders. Records from your country can be played for climate setting. You may have taped your national school children singing their national anthem or a Christian song; you may have a national give his testimony (3 minutes is sufficient) and you could interpret. The sounds of your country will be appreciated by your audience - camel or donkey bells, native music or musical instruments, sounds in the market place, the Muslim call to prayer, etc.

13. Flannelgraph Board. Although we think of the use of flannelgraph as being limited to work with children, it is very effective with adults.

14. Objects and Curios. You will have curios which you have brought home with you (lion tooth necklace, national newspaper, dolls, skins, wood carvings, cooking utensils, clothing, etc., etc.). These can be a most effective means of

describing your country and work. If the items
are drawn from a box or bag so they cannot be
seen before being described, attention is
heightened. Each article may be placed on a
table after being shown.

15. Models. Miniatures of the real item such as
the buildings on your mission station, the
route from the homeland to your area of service,
etc. These can be created from wood, sand,
cardboard, paper, clay, paper mache, or other
materials. Working models may also be created
and used for demonstrating a Persian water wheel
or the operation of a hydroelectric plant.

16. Exhibits and Displays. These will often be as
explanatory as slides or films. But a great
deal of work must go into them. Be sure they
say something, are self-explanatory, and well
made. Plan on paper what you are trying to
accomplish before putting it into more permanent
form. Make it easy to handle and set up. Be
sure to make good use of color, spacing, light-
ing, location, lettering, and unique items.

17. Dioramas. These are scenes representing the
real thing, shown in a 3-dimensional way in
a shoebox or like container. You can utilize
curios, or objects made of clay or soap. A
bit of the artist and some good ideas are needed
to utilize this form of presentation to its best
advantage. One diorama or a series of them can
be utilized, depending on what you try to get
across to your audience.

18. Dramatizing. A husband and wife, or family
team can dramatically show what life is like on
your field. There is no end to the number of
situations which can be worked out in this
manner. Dressing in national clothes and
utilizing large curios and objects are essential.

19. Puppets. Again we have usually limited the use
of puppets to work with children, but they are
just as effective with adults.

20. People. Having dressed one or more of your audience in national clothing, they can be used to demonstrate some of the traits and customs of your nationals. (Be sure to explain just what you will ask of these people before you dress them and use them as models).

Your audio-visual aids will need to be worked out to suit the size of your audience, the type of meeting, the points you want to stress, and the uniqueness with which you are able to reach your goals. You may wish to utilize several combinations of the forms we have mentioned, or you may be able to come up with new ones of your own. Changing the format of your service will put new life into it, for you and for your listeners. Only be sure that your aids are relevant, visible, portable and subordinate to the message you are striving to get across. Your aids will help to improve your presentation by allowing you to present more statistics, graphic illustrations, concrete details and more vivid "for instances".

In preparation, you will need to analyze what you want to say in order to design the proper aids. You will have more confidence, assurance, authority and poise because good aids multiply your ease of communicating, thus improving your friendliness, enthusiasm and rapport with your hearers. Aids help the hearers and observers by generating curiosity, interest and questions.

If aids are not subordinate to the message you are trying to present, then your lecture becomes a demonstration, and you become nothing but a voice. A good test is to determine that what you have to say would be relevant, meaningful, and interesting if it stood on its own; then use aids to supplement what you are saying.

Visual aids should never be left in plain sight. If they are prepared in advance, keep them covered or hidden until used. Otherwise, it will distract from what you are trying to say. The best aid can be held between the speaker and the audience so that neither is distracted by having to turn aside.

The types of aids available to you are limited only by your imagination and the scope of your message.

12

Question And Answer Sessions

Many times in your meetings you will have an opportunity to answer questions posed by your listeners. This is an informal time when both you and your hearers will feel relaxed, and where you can meet each other's needs.

A question and answer period should not be tacked on the end of a lecture to fill up extra time which you have not been able to fill. It should be announced at the beginning of your program and the amount of time to be devoted to it should be stated. Listeners should be invited to note on paper those items about which they would like further information so they will be prepared when the after-session is opened to them. Often when the question period is announced after the speaker has finished, the audience is so unprepared that it takes several minutes to get them into the mood, and then almost always when they warm up and enter in, the time has expired and they still do not have the knowledge they had hoped to obtain.

There is little preparation you can do for this type of session. Most questions will be concerned with the country, culture, people, language and work to which you have gone. You should be prepared to state facts concerning the political trends, the opportunity for workers, the Christian population, the Missions working in your area, numbers of missionaries, problems young people face, etc. Most of the questions will be

relatively simple and your specialized knowledge will
be sufficient in most instances.

There are several factors to keep in mind during
this type of session:

1. Getting started. If people do not have ques-
    tions, seem restless and anxious to get away,
    close the meeting and let them go. On the
    other hand, if they feel inhibited or shy, make
    them feel at ease. There may be occasions
    where someone will be previously "planted"
    with a question in the event folks are slow to
    speak up. This will sometimes get things
    moving if the "plant" is not too contrived
    or obvious.

2. Make sure that questions are heard and under-
    stood and that your answer is heard. Speak
    directly to the point without side-tracking.

3. Occasionally a person will ask a personal or
    "loaded" question, trying to corner you. Answer
    tactfully, "unloading" it by the best means
    possible. You may get complex questions
    requiring several answers. Divide it and
    simplify it as much as possible.

4. Answer as directly as possible, back up your
    statements, if necessary, don't be afraid to
    take a stand, and don't be afraid ever to
    say, "I don't know" if you honestly do not
    have the answer. People are willing to accept
    this answer. Never gloss over or try to make
    up or venture a guess in order to appear to
    have expertise in your field. If you do give
    ideas which may not be valid, be sure to tell
    your audience it is only your guess.

5. Keep the session moving. Let questions be
    asked from several sections of the group. Try
    not to let this lead to a monologue between
    you and one other person. Involve the whole
    group.

6. Why not try throwing out a question to your
    audience such as "How would you feel if . . . ",
    "What would you do . . .", "What are your
    feelings toward . . .", "How would you solve . .",
    "Suppose . . ."

7. Don't let the session drag on ad infinitum and
    ad nauseum.

8. Don't close the session with silence. Many times
    speakers will ask for more questions when there
    are none. After a lapse of nothingness, he
    turns to the pastor, nods, and the session is
    abruptly finished. When the questions are
    over, try to give some sort of summary, challenge,
    or other effective statement which will tie
    loose ends together, and also open the door for
    folks to approach you following the service.

Questions from the audience indicate effectively
whether they were merely casual, uninterested observers,
or active participants, involved in your ministry.
This feedback information can also help you the next
time you speak, for you can incorporate some of the
material about which folks seemed especially interested.
Because you are so close to the situation, it is sometimes difficult to choose what may be most interesting
to those who will hear you. Questions help you to meet
their needs, and in turn help to meet *your* needs.

13

Missionary Conferences

If you are in a mission which sends you on tour,
you may be involved *only* in conference sessions,
perhaps as little as 2 days, or as many as 8 days in
one location. Others of you will, during the course
of furlough, be invited to participate in one or
more conferences.

Looking at it casually, there will seem to be
little difference in providing a single service or
a week of conference - but let's look at it in more
detail.

In your initial letter of invitation, several
facts should be stated, i.e., the name of the parti-
cipating church(es), name of the pastor, name of your
contact person (if other than the pastor), dates of
the conference, location, theme of the conference,
when you are expected to speak, to what groups,
whether a display or literature table will need to be
provided by you, what financial arrangements will be
made for you and whether audio-visuals are requested,
and if so, what equipment will be provided for you.
(If this information is not included, write to the
inviting church requesting further details).

Your responsibility will be to prepare messages,
varying in length, geared to various age groups,
and growing out of the Conference theme. You will
also fit your audio-visuals into the program to expand
your presentations, but still fitting in with the overall theme. Your display will emphasize the theme again.

Although seldom mentioned specifically, pastors always
appreciate this emphasis.

Remember that you may be the only missionary at a
given conference, or you may be one of sixty. In either
case, your presentations must be so vital and unique
that they will be remembered. To do this, you do
not have to be a dynamic, world-renowned personality.
You have only to be enthused about your area of service
and, by some means, make your enthusiasm contagious.
Some will ask "How is this possible? Who wants to
hear how I build a church, or how I repair the mission
cars, or how I keep the press running, or how I enter-
tain at tea?" Do you have the assurance that your
work is vital to your mission's outreach? Are you
assured that you are in God's perfect will? Do you
have any contact with that which is happening in your
area? Do you see the need for others to give their
lives in service to the Lord for just the thing you
are doing? Perhaps your satisfaction in the service of
the King cannot come from the fact that you are winning
nationals to Christ and building them up in the faith.
But surely, as a member of the team, you *do* have a
share in all that is accomplished. It is possible
that you, in your supporting ministry, can be identified with by many of those who will hear you speak,
for they, too, are in a supportive role by their gifts
and prayers on behalf of those who are out on the front
lines. You, more than other missionaries, can encourage
and challenge those who can help through use of just
ordinary talents. You can challenge men and women to
short-term service. You can lay before them the need
for retired folks to volunteer for a year or two of
ministry. Surely you can speak in depth of the type
of prayer partners which are needed to uphold the work
of the ministry. You can give a clear presentation as
to where missionary dollars go and how they are used.
Your personal testimony will be used in a wonderful way
as you ask God to make it pertinent to your listeners.
You can do much to make people in the homeland realize
that *missionaries are ordinary Christian people, facing
the same problems and temptations with which folks in
the homeland have to deal*. You can gently lower the
missionary from his pedestal and show him to be merely
the Ambassador of Christ which God intends for Him to
be. You can be a living proof that faithfulness to God

is every Christian's foremost responsibility.

So, if you are not the world's greatest speaker, if you feel your ministry is obscured because of the things which are so daily, and you are on the platform with men and women who have worked in more difficult fields, can make their audience weep over the sad state of the poor women and orphans, or who can tell story upon story of scores of conversions - remember that those missionaries will be respected, and looked up to, and admired, and yet in the end, the listeners may actually be better able to identify with you and your work, because they, themselves, are involved in this type of service.

Now many of you will be "born speakers". Words may flow easily and sincerely. You can hold the attention of your group. You can present your field and your ministry in an unforgettable way. You are creative and your presentations are well-planned and long remembered. You are in an evangelistic ministry or a church planting position. You are involved in many areas of the work. You are outgoing and being in an administrative position, you have a far better overall view of the work being accomplished in your field, and throughout all the fields of your Mission. You speak with authority, know your fellow-workers intimately, and enjoy your deputation ministry. You can present a challenge that produces response. Be grateful that God has given you special talents.

Missionary conferences are a good opportunity to present your field and work in depth. You can build upon previous sessions. You can also learn from listening to other speakers, viewing others' visual aids and displays. You are with the church group for a sustained period of time, and can, therefore, come to know them while they come to know you.

Missionary conferences can also have drawbacks. It may mean dividing a family for this period of time. Very few churches, using a number of missionaries in a conference, invite children to attend. This means, unless you have friends or relatives in the area, children must be left with others at home, or one parent stays home to babysit while the other goes to the

conference. Conferences are usually scheduled for a
time when children are normally in school. Thus some
churches never meet the "other half" of the missionaries
they support.

Then, too, conferences can be very wearying to
those who tire easily. Not only are there the planned
meetings at which you are to speak, but on the spur
of the moment you may be asked to say "a word" many
times. Extra meetings may be scheduled at the last
minute. Other churches may request your appearance
during the conference week. Informal Home Bible Classes
may ask you to attend and speak. Perhaps you will
find yourself being asked for an interview by the
local newspapers, radio or television. On some
occasions you may be asked to teach classes at the
local Christian or Public Schools. You are expected to
be at the Men's breakfast, the Women's Missionary Tea,
the Young People's banquet, the daily noon luncheons
at a local cafeteria, the evening pot-luck suppers with
the members of the church, and the daily afternoon
prayer meetings. The church somehow feels you are
their property 24 hours a day and you are expected to
abide by their schedule - or be in danger of losing
support or being dropped entirely.

If you are physically able to keep up with the
schedule, you will, of course, do your best to comply.
But if you are not able to do so, be very frank with
the pastor of your host church, share your limitations,
ask for time to rest, if need be. Most pastors will be
understanding of your needs once they understand the
situation.

Since churches often prepare for their conference
for a full year, and it becomes the highlight of the
church year, when the time actually arrives, they want
the most and best they can get from you. Try to understand their position. It will be difficult to keep up
such heavy schedules conference after conference. There
must be understanding on both sides. Fit in as much as
possible. If you must have a day away by yourself,
contact the proper authority and get permission to do
so. A great deal will be expected of you. Try to
take it in stride. Refresh yourself as much as possible
through the ministry of others.

By all means, do not go on to your next meeting or conference and brag or complain about how hard you were worked in a previous engagement. Whether condoning or condemning, you are placing your present ministry in jeopardy. So take your conferences as they come, enjoy them to the full, rest as much as possible, prepare and pray as much as necessary, and commit it all to the Lord.

Try not to be disappointed if you are in a conference for a week and receive no financial support as a result. This often happens. Yet God will supply your needs. And you may never know, this side of glory, of those whose hearts were touched by your messages and who have prayed for you daily, although they have never written you or sent you a gift.

When you are competing with many missionaries from many fields, never try to outdo them with sensational or gory tales, jokes, sympathetic appeals, or by trying to "ape" them or their techniques. As in every presentation, be strictly honest, present yourself, your Board, your field and your work as you see them and leave the service with the Lord to speak to the minds and hearts of people. Human persuasion is seldom successful. Stretching points to make them sound clever or productive may be picked up and examined and compared with the truth, to your utter dismay and embarrassment. Make no statements and give no examples which you cannot back up with evidence. And unless you are sure your facts are correct, better omit them. Hearsay evidence will not do.

Conferences can be a great learning experience. You meet folks from several areas of the world. Talk with them about their problems and how they solve them. Find out about their ministries. Discover recent trends in their policies. Learn about their fields. Discuss unique methods of missionary endeavor. Share your field with them. Missionaries can become very cloistered, knowing very little about the world of missions other than the work on their station or among their tribe. At conferences you can take in as well as giving out.

And at many conferences there is sufficient time for rest and relaxation. Happy is the missionary who is invited to a conference in Florida during November or February! Time for boating, fishing, swimming, sightseeing and sunbathing are offered while friends in the north are turning up the heat and shoveling snow! There *are* compensations for conference speakers!

If you are a missionary in the homeland, your ministry can be made as exciting to your hearers as that of anyone working anywhere in the world. Your service is on equal with any other missionary. It has as much challenge, it produces as many results, and it needs as many workers as God can supply through those whom you have an opportunity to contact. You are, in no way, "among the least of these".

14

Honesty In Presentations

Missionaries are not dishonest people. They are Christians who have felt the call of God upon their lives for service in a full-time commitment either at home or abroad. They have been honest enough to admit to this call and have responded to it. Why, then, must we caution about honesty?

Admittedly, every individual sees a situation from a personal viewpoint. This is why witnesses at the scene of an accident give conflicting testimony. This is what makes debating teams function. This is what gives personality and flavor to human beings. But, in reality, it marks us as liberal or conservative, democratic or autocratic, right or wrong, broad-minded or biased, good or bad.

Sometimes in stressing a point, it is easy to alter statistics, create situations which are more fable than fact, and give false impressions of what is really happening on the field. Part of this is demanded by church groups. People in the homeland do not always understand why one missionary comes home boasting of thousands of converts and scores of churches while another comes home to confess the conversion of three souls, two of whom have backslidden and turned back to their former religion because of the pressures brought to bear upon them. If these two missionaries are scheduled to speak on the same platform or at the same conference, it is a temptation to make the one convert appear to be a giant of the faith, witnessing without reservation, and surely a jewel for the missionary's crown. Because facts have to be focused on such a small area of the work in order to magnify the one convert, many false impressions can be given.

For those who work in out-of-the-way places, it is easy to dwell on one tiny fragment of a small tribe, which is not especially typical of the rest of the country in which you work but you neglect to mention this. Urban workers speak of the city and neglect the rural work.

When showing slides, try to avoid the expression, "This is a typical . . ." It is confusing to supporting churches when you show a grass hut as being typical of your country and the next missionary from your area shows a brick house, declaring it is typical. The truth is, that depending upon what area you happen to be in, a certain scene is typical. But it may be entirely atypical when considering the entire country of which you are a part. Show your pictures and explain them, but try not to show "typical shots".

A missionary is, of course, supposed to be desperately unhappy in the homeland, and hardly able to wait for the day of return to his people. This may or may not be true. If you are enjoying the refreshment and rest of furlough days, you don't have to try to convince people you are out of your element away from the mission field. If you stress your desire to be back on the field openly and too often, it can embarrass the people or churches among whom you are presently fellowshipping, for they will feel that you find a lack in them. On the other hand, it could show a lack in you. Perhaps by stressing your longing to be back on the field, you are trying to convince yourself that you really feel that way when you don't. Analyze your attitude toward this matter and be sure that you honestly and con- scientiously miss your work, your co-workers, and the nationals with whom you serve, or say nothing.

Some missionaries feel that when asked, even pri- vately, if they have a need for additional support or equipment, their reply should be that "God has always met my needs, and He will continue to do so." This is your side of the picture, but this is no answer to one, who in all sincerity, wishes to enter into financial fellowship with a missionary. If, indeed, you have everything you need for support, travel and equipment, is it possible that you would appreciate a magazine subscription (Christian, general or technical), or some item of equipment which you hadn't mentioned to anyone, but had previously hoped to be able to obtain? It is not strictly honest to say you have everything you need if there is something you feel would be helpful in your ministry. If asked, give a truthful answer.

How do you describe your new country? What do you mention about the people? How do you speak about their present religions? Missionaries often give the impression that the natives lined the streets when they arrived, waiting with open arms to welcome these Christian workers, ready to give up their unsatisfying religion to accept the foreigner's good news of Jesus Christ. Is it wrong to confess to your prayer partners in the homeland that your arrival went unheralded (as did your recent departure); in fact, there was open opposition to your intrusion, and the "natives" were completely happy and satisfied with their own religion?

Why do missionaries insist on telling only of the victories they have encountered? Were there no defeats? Are you really telling it like it is, or are some facts hidden behind a facade of strength in and devotion to the Lord? Is He, in truth, the only thing that matters to you? Has it been easy to go where He has led? To say what He would have you say? To do what He asked you to do? To be all that He wanted you to be?

Or perhaps you have dwelt on the despairing negatives and you have left your audiences with such a dark view of the work that they feel sorry for you and are assured that only failure can result from missionary efforts in your area.

A wise missionary doesn't tell eveything he knows. He doesn't condemn his mission or his fellow-workers, or his own inability to adjust and get along with people. Discernment must be exercised along with honesty in deciding what should be said, and what should not be stated.

If you are involved in a missionary conference in a large city church, it is very possible that there will be one or more nationals from your field in your congregation. If you are not aware of their presence, you may give a very biased view of their country. If you sense their presence, you will do everything in your power to speak the truth in love and present a well-rounded picture. You can never be sure such people will not be among your hearers, so be prepared always to give a fair, accurate and truthful picture of your work.

If a missionary asks another missionary, "What is your greatest problem on the field?", the answer 9 times out of 10 will be, "Getting along with people." If a lay person asks the same question, he can expect to hear "Lack of time", "Dishonest servants", "Lack of adequate transportation", "Illiteracy of the people", etc., etc. With whom are we honest? What was YOUR greatest problem on the field? Do not prayer partners deserve to know the truth so they can better pray intelligently?

Let's not try to fool ourselves in this matter of misrepresentation of facts. It can be dangerous and devastating. Honesty is, after all, the best policy.

15

Courtesy And Gratitude

To remind missionaries of the need for gratitude and courtesy may appear to be unnecessary. Yet it affects so many vital relationships, it seems appropriate to emphasize it again and again. Unfortunately, there are those who feel they deserve the funds they receive from individuals and supporting churches since "the laborer is worthy of his hire." Therefore, little is said or done to show appreciation for the gifts which supply every need according to God's promise. If a supporter tires of this attitude of ingratitude, support may be dropped. By this it is not meant to be implied that missionaries should thank people merely that their support will be maintained at the proper level. This would be adding insult to injury. One could rationalize and determine that tithe money is due the Lord, and therefore, there is really no personal involvement just because it happens to be designated for your support. A good test of your appreciation for those who support you comes when, if you are under a mission which pools its support funds, you receive only 50% of your normal salary allowance. Do you fuss or complain? Do you find it more difficult to get through the month? Do you have to go without a few items you had planned on purchasing? Without a doubt, some thought is given to the fact that you have had an insufficient salary. But, on the other hand, when your full support is given month after month, are you as knowingly grateful as you were openly complaining? Think about this, and then be grateful for those who faithfully support you. Some of them will invest many thousands of dollars in you and your ministry through the years. They would like some response from their investment. If you are too busy to say "thank you", you are too busy! Now you are home does not relieve you of the responsibility of thanking your supporters for their continuing gifts.

You will be asking for meetings in various churches, or will be invited by pastors to take services during your furlough. If you are to speak at an evening service some distance from your home, it is never out of place to ask if overnight accommodations can be arranged. Along with this, be sure to specify how many individuals this will involve, along with the age and sex of children who may accompany you. If a church offers accommodations, but you have made previous arrangements, be very frank about explaining this. It is usually good, however, to stay with folks from the church you are visiting if at all possible since it gives you a closer tie with them. But, it may be necessary to stay with relatives or friends in the area whom you would otherwise not be able to visit during furlough.

When staying in homes providing hospitality for you, be as considerate as possible of your hosts. Don't make a shambles of your room by hanging, draping and dropping clothing, etc. on the bed, chairs and floor. If space is provided, hang clothing in the closet. Many articles can remain in your suitcase. If an iron is needed, ask your hostess for one and be sure to use it on her ironing board, not on her dresser. If you need to wash out a few articles, ask where you should hang them. Again, don't hang a wet shirt or dress in your room and let it drip all over the floor or rug. If you must have food snacks in your room, don't get the crumbs on the floor or in the bed. And in the morning, be sure to make your bed, or strip it at the request of your hostess.

If you are expected to arrive at a certain hour, and you are delayed en route, let your hosts know. Be sure to find out what arrangements have been made for your meals. If your host does not tell you what time breakfast is to be, ask. Be sure to carry an alarm clock with you when you travel. It is an essential part of furlough equipment. If you are arriving by plane or train and must be met, try to arrive and depart at reasonable hours to accommodate those responsible for your transportation.

Never complain about food which is served to you. If there must be restrictions in your diet, specify this in your original letter telling the time of your arrival. No one objects to leaving onions or salt out of their food, but no one condones complaints about items when there was no idea that these could not be tolerated favorably by you. Of course, if parsnips are served, and you just can't "go them", it's always polite to leave them untouched on your plate if they are served to you, or to pass them by if you have a choice. The usual complaint of furlough folks is that too many people feed them too well too often. If you are a guest in one home at noon and in another home for the evening meal, normally the family will serve their big meal when you are with them. This does not mean, however, that you must eat a huge meal at each sitting. Discipline in the matter of eating must be exercised. It will be a struggle because most things will be very tempting, and some of them you will not have been able to get on the field. Nevertheless, one helping should be the rule.

If you are travelling with your children, be sure your children are suitable houseguests. They should not be allowed to roam throughout the home, picking up and handling every item in sight. Small children cannot be expected to sit for four hours with their hands folded. Be sure to take games, coloring books, dolls, etc., for them to play with. If the children are undisciplined, you'd better plan not to bring them.

Most families who accommodate you, knowing your children will be with you, will make them feel at home. They may even spoil them. It is your privilege to specify the limits allowed.

In some cases, families will give up their own bedroom, or ship their children off to the neighbors to make room for you and your family. Be sincerely appreciative of all they do for you. Above all, remember that these people are sharing the best that they have with you. It is never in order to boast to them that

"the last church we went to provided accommodations in
a local Motel and it was fantastic." Or "a family in
one of the churches we visited let us stay in their
beautiful home for a week. They let us use their
Cadillac, and the kids sure enjoyed the swimming pool
and the boat on the lake." Nor, by the way, do you
ever mention in meetings your visits to other churches,
criticizing or commending them, nor do you describe
people in those churches. Even though it may be
hundreds of miles distant, someone in the congregation may just happen to know of whom or what you are
speaking. When you are in a given community, your
attention should be focused positively on the people
there. Sides should never be taken in church disputes.
Controversial subjects should not be discussed.

If you are taken to a restaurant for a meal, unless
you are certain your hosts mean for you to do so, try
to refrain from ordering the $8.50 steak. If possible,
try to determine what they are going to eat, and limit
yourself to that approximate price range. Some
hosts will insist upon the most expensive meal, and
if you are in agreement with their choice of the main
dish, let them order it for you. But in other cases,
if you do not know your hosts, it is far better to
order what you really like in a lower price category.
If your children are with you, be sure to order something they enjoy. Order a child's plate if a full
meal contains too much food. And never discourage a
hamburger or hot dog if this is what the child enjoys
most.

If you are invited to a church, and already have
other meetings in the area, be sure to tell the pastors
of each church. Sometimes you will arrive in an area
for one meeting and the church will ask you to stay for
another service. The courtesy of telling your plans
beforehand will help your host church to plan more adequately and intelligently.

You have been out of the country for quite some time.
You now live "out there" in a land where people are
brutally frank and outspoken. Remember when you return
home that it is not at all polite to admire someone's
suit or dress and then ask how much they paid for it.
Try to remember the courtesies of your own culture.

Some of you will have friends who send out your prayer letters for you. This involves keeping your address list updated, preparing envelopes, getting your letter typed, printed, stuffed, sealed, stamped and mailed. If you've been taking this friend or these friends for granted, be sure to put out your own letters during furlough - especially if you have over 500 on your mailing list. You will discover how much work and expense is involved, and it will make you appreciate this service to a far greater extent. Be sure to give an indication as to how many times a year you expect to send out a letter. Also, if your friend should be moving, save your letter until the move is completed. Never send a letter less than a month before Christmas and expect it to be in the mail before the holiday. Be helpful and courteous in these details.

If someone has offered to pay for your prayer letters, you may find a church or an organization which will do the actual sending. Even in this case, don't send a letter every month just because someone else is paying for it. Four times a year is maximal. Once a year is minimal.

If, during furlough, you have special favors done for you, be sure to give a token of appreciation to the one(s) responsible by means of a gift or a sincere note of thanks. But do not overlook these blessings bestowed upon you. Some of these favors might include care by a doctor, dentist or lawyer; discounts in stores; mechanical work on your car; housing; food; use of a gasoline credit card; courses at local educational institutions; admission to refresher workshops and seminars; toys for the children; gifts of equipment for yourself or your mission, etc.

Each time word reaches you that support or personal gifts have been received for your account, write a brief card or note of thanks.

No one is obliged to support you, but their willingness to do so should receive a response of gratitude from you. Perhaps close friends have a part in your support. Don't neglect to thank them, too. It's even easier to take their gifts for granted than those received from strangers.

Always thank a church publicly for allowing you the
privilege of being with them. People like to be appreciated. It takes little effort, but it can encourage
an otherwise disinterested group.

Sometimes Christians expect more from the preacher's
kids than they do from other children. They also seem
to expect more from missionaries than from other Christian
Although we may have gone too far in that direction,
nevertheless, it stands to reason that missionaries need
both to receive and to give a fair share of gratitude
and courtesy. If these do not come naturally to you,
be sure to work at it. Without them, your furlough
ministry will be thwarted and unfruitful. With them,
people will be attracted to you and the Lord will be
glorified in your life.

16

Communication With The Field

During your furlough time, it is extremely important to keep up with happenings on the field. If you are in a leadership position, this is imperative, since you may be responsible for making important decisions affecting the work on the field. If you are not in an administrative capacity, you will want to keep the field informed concerning your definite plans for return and ideas you would like to investigate. Depending upon the type of control within your Board, you will be expected to comply with orders from the field and the Home Office, or be able to write very freely concerning your goals for your next term of service. You should keep in contact with your co-workers to receive up-to-date news from your area. You may wish to correspond with nationals.

Correspondence will never take the place of actually being in a situation. It can be very biased and one-sided. If you are on the scene, you know all the "little" things that surround each happening affecting you. But when such events are put on paper by a fellow-missionary or a national, they can appear warped and twisted; overly optimistic or pessimistic. You must take into consideration that letters can only give you a general, one-person opinion about any given situation.

Your own role in communication should be to encourage and enlighten. No matter how you think your station must be run in your absence, be sure to give a fair

amount of freedom in the work. Furlough time should
not be a continual worry about how poorly your station
is being handled in your absence. Do not write remarks
to nationals which degrade the work or the workers. Do
not try to have them lean heavily upon you, but encourage them to trust the Lord, each other and their
missionary partners.

If you have grudges against anything or anyone, do
not let your feelings out on paper to avoid a direct
confrontation with the person or persons involved.
Communications via the written word are easily misinterpreted.

There are countries today where letters can, at
the discretion of the ruling government, be censored
or confiscated. There must be a great deal of discretion used in written communications, especially in
troubled countries of the world. Your personal feelings
even your ideas of your country's feelings about the
land in which you work - should not be stated. Criticism
of your adopted country, no matter how slight, should
be avoided. When this type of information falls into
the wrong hands, it can cause missions to be in jeopardy
of losing their entry privileges.

Even though a national may be a very close friend
in whom you feel you may confide, never write in
criticism of your mission or its missionaries. Even
among strong Christian national believers, it is a
temptation to destroy the effectiveness of the ministry
of the foreigner. Nationalism can be very strong to
these believers. They may have every right to believe
that their own people can do the job as well as, if not
better than, the missionary.

On the other hand, do not ignore your national
brethren just because you are away from them. You can
continue to have a ministry to them through this means
of communication. It may be difficult for you to understand their language. It may be even harder for you to
write a meaningful letter in their language. But this
contact can be profitable as they understand you have
not forgotten them even though you have parted for a
while.

Many of our problems come from lack of communication — even when we are in a group and can speak face to face. Often very serious situations can be avoided if you will take the time to keep in touch with the field. If you are not a writer, become one. Determine to become involved. Perhaps you need to clarify an issue, or receive clarification of an event or policy. Perhaps you merely want some word concerning a project you began or how the building is progressing, or how many attended the deeper life conference.

By all means, do not lose contact with the field while you are away from it. You may not be told all the struggles and problems, but you can obtain information. You do not have to become personally involved in other's trials except through the ministry of prayer. Seek honestly to have this continuing fellowship.

Some of you may be fortunate enough to have a friend or neighbor who is a ham radio operator. If it is possible to contact your field in this way, ask for the privilege of doing so through your friend. Although business matters cannot be handled in this fashion, it is a convenient way to get routine news items concerning what's going on in your work, on your field and at your station.

17

Prayer Cards

When you were first accepted by your Board, you hastened to have prayer cards printed for distribution. This is no less necessary during your furlough period. You have changed! You may have had additions to your family. Interested prayer partners and supporters will appreciate an up-dated reminder. And while you are having a picture taken for your prayer reminder cards, be sure to obtain a copy for the Home Office of your Mission. These are often used in the annual prayer bulletin, or in other literature. Some missions use a picture in their periodical when you return to the field. Many Home Offices keep a bulletin board with pictures of missionaries. Perhaps you have noted annual prayer bulletins from other mission (or perhaps your own) where some of the pictures, even of the administrative and home staff, have not been changed for ten years. Don't let this be the case with you.

When preparing your prayer card, be sure it contains the following information:

1. Your picture

2. Your name

3. Your address (on the field)

4. Your Mission's name

5. Your Mission's address

6. Where you will be serving

It is possible that you know exactly what your work will be upon your return to the field. If so, this can be included in print or by means of a line drawing or graphic art.

As upon your acceptance, your prayer card will need to be well-planned. The color(s), type of stock (heavy, light, coated), style (wallet size, bookmark, 2- or 3-fold, stand-up, special cut such as praying hands, airplane, nurses cap, map) formal invitation type, flat, printed on one or both sides, must be decided. Do you want a Scripture verse imprinted? A map? In these considerations, remember that you are striving to produce something that will cause people to think specifically of YOU and YOUR ministry. It must be uniquely yours. Set your goals as to their purpose(s). Find a good printer who will work with you to communicate exactly what you desire through the finished product.

Perhaps you have proper facilities on your field to have the cards printed before you reach the homeland. If so, you may wish to enclose them with a letter from the field announcing your forthcoming furlough. Or you may wish to carry them with you for distribution in your early meetings. This would be most appropriate if you have only a short furlough. Some Boards have a set pattern for their prayer cards. If so, it may be necessary for you to correspond with the Home Office to make arrangements. If a recent picture is sent to them, they may be able to have the reminders ready for you upon arrival at home.

You must decide on the method of distribution of your reminders. Consider:

1. Enclosing one in a prayer letter sent upon your arrival in the homeland.

2. Put them on the display or literature table in your meetings for general distribution.

3. Have people sign up for one, allowing you a confirming letter to them after your departure from their presence, enclosing the card. This is good follow-up procedure and maintains an otherwise casual contact.

4. Send them in letters to pastors requesting speaking engagements.

5. Enclose one in each thank-you letter written to those who provide hospitality during your tour of deputation.

6. Give them only to those who promise prayer and financial support.

7. Send them in a letter in a general mailing just prior to or upon your departure for the field.

You will want to leave a supply of cards at your Home Office. There are occasions when churches request the names of missionaries for whom they can pray or in whom they can have a financial interest. The Board will then be able to supply a reminder of you which helps cement their decision. Supporting churches will sometimes request a number of cards for a missionary conference or special emphasis meeting. Always leave at least a dozen copies with your Home Office. If you have a packet left over when you return to the field, leave them, too. You have no further use for them. If your Board cannot use or store them, they may discard them after a reasonable time, but in the meanwhile, they are available if requested.

In many instances, the cost of prayer cards is a legitimate expense which can be taken from the work account set up for you. Some Boards take the expense from General Funds if it is mission policy to require cards. For a few, the expense will be borne from the support account, personal funds, or by the gift of an interested friend.

Prayer cards are an effective communicative aid in maintaining the interest of God's people in you and your ministry. Distribute them carefully and prayerfully.

18

Legal Matters

Be sure that all your papers are in order before leaving the field, since your return may depend upon this. Some countries allow you a "No objection to return" document. Others demand it. All income tax should be cleared, residence papers updated, health certificates signed, passports in order, visaes renewed and departure papers duly signed by the appropriate officials. This is all very time consuming, but absolutely essential.

Upon arrival home there are papers which need to be checked and brought up to date in some cases.

Your WILL should be considered. Perhaps you went to the field single and are now coming home married with a family. Codicils may need to be added, or a new will made (the latter probably being the better method). Some Boards have a mission lawyer, or a member of the Advisory Board or Reference Council who may undertake to provide this service to missionaries. For some, there may need to be changes in beneficiaries or executor. If, for some reason, you went to the field originally with no official will on file, be sure to take care of this matter at once. For those of you with children who are not yet of age, it is important that you specify a guardian in the event they should be orphaned.

Consider your INSURANCE policy(ies). Do you have living beneficiaries named? Do you want to change the beneficiary? Do you have sufficient insurance to meet your needs? This is an item worthy of a heart-to-heart talk with a knowledgeable insurance company agent.

If you gave your POWER OF ATTORNEY to an individual when you departed for the field, have you been satisfied with your choice, or should a change be made? In any event it should be given to one in whom you trust so that legal matters concerning you can be cared for in your absence without the delay, bother and possibility of loss which comes from sending legal papers to the field to be signed and returned.

Look at your PASSPORT to see when it expires. It is usually far easier to have it renewed in the homeland than on the field.

VISAS AND ENTRANCE PAPERS will probably be cared for by your Board at an appropriate time so they can be cleared before your furlough is finished. Early attention to this important matter will expedite your return on time. Visaes for many countries are being delayed, some withheld in these days. Pray much that God will overrule in the obtaining of these vital affidavits.

You will probably have questions concerning SOCIAL SECURITY and INCOME TAX. If your Home Office cannot answer your questions concerning these matters, be sure to have a conference with your nearest Social Security Office and/or your Internal Revenue Service Agency.

If you have neglected to keep up a DRIVER'S LICENSE in the homeland, do not drive until it is legal for you to do so. Some States allow the renewal in spite of a lapse. Others may require a written examination and/or a road test. Many renewals now also require a picture for identification and a sight and hearing test. Check with your local Office of Motor Vehicles concerning these matters.

PROFESSIONAL LICENSES must also be kept in force. If, through error or carelessness, you have allowed your license to lapse, be sure to find out the procedure for becoming reinstated.

Your HEALTH CARD will continue to be a constant companion to your passport. Keep your immunizations up-to-date.

If you had no need for a BANK ACCOUNT upon your initial departure for the field, you may wish to open one now. It may be best to have your Home Office treasurer's name on your account. In this way he can transact business at your request. It is especially important if you need to pay bills, purchase items to be sent to you or you wish to make deposits toward your children's education, etc.

It is best to have a copy of your BIRTH CERTIFICATE, ORDINATION, COMMISSIONING, and/or RECOMMISSIONING PAPER and MARRIAGE CERTIFICATE (if applicable) available.

Maintaining all of these legal matters in order is essential. Check on them periodically and make sure all is properly cared for.

19

Medical And Dental Work

Most missions require their missionaries to have a complete physical examination, including lab work, just before leaving the field (if there is a good medical set-up in your mission) or immediately upon arrival in the homeland by an appointed mission doctor or your own physician with reports being sent to your Home Office. It is a testimony to the grace of God that these reports are often remarkably normal. If, however, there is a problem of dysentery, malaria, or other physical maladjustment, prompt attention can be given. Other problems may be discovered, too, which will require extensive treatment or surgery. Discovering this at the beginning of furlough helps in planning for the days and weeks ahead. This is especially essential for those who have chosen the short term, short furlough.

Although the physical examination is usually a must, a dental examination may not be required. For your own peace of mind and the preservation of your teeth, be sure to have dental needs cared for early in your furlough with a final check just before leaving for the field once again. Good dentists are few and far between on many fields unless you are stationed in a large, modern city.

Unless your Board is responsible for your medical and dental bills, you will be shocked at the expense of

a complete physical or a partial plate. If you receive
$140 per month for salary and having a tooth capped
costs $250, you may be tempted to give up in despair.
Your bills may run to $2000 for a family of four in a
very short time, and your medical insurance covers
none of it. You may be tempted to try to get a better
price somewhere else, but unless a Christian doctor
or dentist is willing to provide such services at cost
or as a contribution, it is probably wisest to get
the best care for the price asked. It will mean truly
trusting the Lord for funds to cover the expense, but
He never says "I will provide all your needs, except
medical and dental expenses."

It is always in order to ask professional men if
they allow a discount to those in the ministry. Many
of them have such a policy. But never demand this from
them. And in good faith, pay your bills as promptly
as possible. No doctor or dentist complains if you
make arrangements beforehand to pay $5 or $10 per
month on your bill. But be sure to follow through on
your part of the bargain. It may be necessary for
you to make arrangements for payment through your Home
Office by having them withhold the required amount from
your support each month to be sent on by them to fulfill
your obligation.

If an operation is necessary and you carry appropriate insurance, the doctor may be willing to charge
only the amount covered by insurance for his services.
Again, do not demand this, and if you are left with a
large personal bill, it must be cared for by you by
the best arrangement possible. Professional men deserve
to be paid for their services and it is up to you to
honor their bills with payment.

Those of you with children will be tempted to get
their teeth checked by an orthodontist. Remember, however, that the straightening of teeth can be a long
process. Before allowing braces to be used, check to
see how often they have to be checked and approximately
how long they will be needed, as well as the cost of the
entire project. Parents and children appreciate straight
teeth, but other factors must be taken into consideration. How long is your furlough? Is the work worth the
time and expense involved? Will it make a major improve-

ment? Is it a necessary procedure? Is there opportunity
for follow-up in the field to which you are assigned?

Some individuals put off required treatment because
(1) they are too busy; (2) it is too expensive; (3) they
feel it isn't essential; (4) they're scared. (What will
the biopsy show? What if the anesthesia affects me
adversely? What if it's worse than it appears? I don't
like to take medicine). None of these reasons seem
valid when you measure the preventive or curative
factors of treatment with a long and physically successful missionary career. And certainly your children
deserve the very best treatment in this regard.

Some of you are frail and always will be. Others
are strong and feel nothing will ever change that. But
it is the responsibility of each individual to look to
his Heavenly Father for health and strength in the greatest degree possible. Your body is the temple of the Holy
Spirit. It is this body which makes it possible for
you to take the gospel to those to whom God has sent you.
Make sure, then, this temple is in the best possible
condition physically, mentally and emotionally, as well
as spiritually.

20

Records, Reports
And Financial Affairs

Paper work is an essential part of the present
world system, and missionaries, too, must comply with
the rules. It is time consuming, sometimes frus-
trating, often monotanous. But it is still necessary.
Therefore, the best way to attack it is to keep your
records and reports up-to-date. If you let a month
lapse and then try to figure out how many miles you
travelled, how much toll was paid, how much was received in your meetings, etc., it will be an impossible
job. The easiest way to keep accurate records, of
course, is to carry a small notebook in your pocket,
purse, or the glove compartment of your car. Jot down
pertinent information when it happens. Then it is
simply a matter of transferring this information to
report sheets supplied by your mission, or to plain
typing paper. JUST A REMINDER! *Make someone very
happy. TYPE YOUR REPORTS, IF POSSIBLE!* Otherwise,
be sure to write or print legibly.

Most missions ask for a monthly report of meetings,
expenditures and offerings. Whenever you send checks
to the Home Office to be receipted, be sure to identify
specifically where the receipt should be sent, i.e.,
name, full address, zip code, and name of the church
or group. Be sure it is properly designated, also.
Always ask for this essential information whenever you
are presented with funds. You may wish to send the
offerings to the office as soon as you receive them
rather than waiting to send your monthly report. This

assures the donors of prompt receipting. It also means you are not responsible for a large number of checks. Never send cash to the Home Office. Usually you will have a checking account while on furlough. If possible, deposit the cash and send your personal check to cover it. Or you may wish to use the cash and send the check from your account.

When sending reports to the office, be sure the amount of your report and the total of your checks tally. If funds have been expended, write a letter explaining this. There are occasions when money has been used for a legitimate item of equipment, and although it is not available as cash, it must be receipted. Try to avoid a situation of this nature since legally the mission should not receipt funds not passing through its hands. The usual procedure is to send the funds for receipting and ask for a mission check by return mail. If it is imperative that you spend funds, you might send the mission a personal check, asking them to return it by mission check to your account.

Sometimes people give you gifts through the church. In that case, a receipt is sent to the church. If a personal receipt should be issued, indicate this, giving full name, address and zip code of the donor. It is not possible to send a receipt to a donor when the church has already received a receipt for that gift. For income tax purposes, the donor must get evidence from the church, not the mission, in such cases.

If funds are needed for travel, equipment or reimbursement, send a letter, or a form to your Home Office indicating how much is needed and why. Ordinarily you will not be able to receive funds if those funds are not in your account. The only exception would be that support and housing will be given even though the account is in the red, but is is understood that the missionary cannot return to the field until his account is in the black and sufficient support funds have been promised for his coming term of service. (Not every Board makes this exception).

Medical reports should be submitted to the Home Office upon arrival in the homeland. If there are items to be cared for, the missionary will not be allowed to return to the field until he has medical clearance.

If an extension of furlough or leave of absence is anticipated for health, family or educational purposes, be sure to obtain approval from the Home Office well in advance of your previously designated date of return and notify the Field Office. There may also be times when a missionary is assigned to special service in his homeland to fill a need in the Office or in representation. This should have both field and Home Office approval.

In your reports, be sure to give addresses where you may be reached most quickly during furlough. Sometimes this will consist of your tentative itinerary. At times your home address will be the best contact. But it is essential that you apprise the Home Office of your location at all times, for forwarding mail, sending monthly checks and reimbursements, and for emergency purposes.

You will, from time to time, meet those who have a general interest in your mission and will want to be placed on the mailing list to receive mailings. Be sure to obtain the proper title (Mr., Mrs., Miss, Rev., Dr., Prof., etc.), full name, correct address (including Box or Route number where applicable) and correct zip code. Your Home Office will have their files set up by zip code, so this is an essential item. Ordinarily, donors to the mission will receive mission literature on a regular basis.

Mission Offices are usually in the market for articles or news from your field. Don't be afraid to submit copy and pictures for possible publication. Often you will be asked for such information upon your arrival in the homeland.

In your personal report notebook, it is good to make a notation of what you spoke about, what Scripture you used, and what audio-visuals were utilized at each meeting. It is possible that before furlough is over, you may be asked to return to the same church, and how embarrassing it would be to repeat your previous message!

Among reports which are necessary are the prayer or

newsletters. Even though you are at home, it is
essential to keep friends and supporters informed as
to your location, work, needs and prayer requests.
And, of course, these "form" letters will not take the
place of personal "thank you" notes to those who contri-
bute to your support.

Your Home Office will be kept informed as to your
support standing. Before return to the field is approved
a list of all donors and amounts pledged must be sent
to the Office. If support is below par, confer with
your Board concerning it. In most cases today, missions
must insist on minimum support being fully pledged
before return to the field.

If personal gifts are given to you and the donor requests no receipt, they do not have to be reported to
the office. Personal gifts can be receipted, but must
be clearly identified as not being deductible for income
tax purposes.

Usually, if you take a full-time position for your
furlough period, you are allowed (1) to keep the money
you receive from your work for salary and living expenses and not accept monthly allowance from the mission,
or (2) live on your monthly mission allowance, sending
each pay check from your work to be credited to your
account. The latter method is usually used when a
missionary's account is in the red and must be built
up before return to the field, or when a missionary is
mainly self-supporting. It is also employed when a
missionary insists on working rather than becoming
involved in deputation work.

If you are requested to do deputation on behalf of
the mission, you are usually reimbursed for travel, but
funds received from your speaking go to the mission rathe
than to your support account.

If you are planning to visit the Home Office, and
this should be a requirement, let the staff know of your
arrival well in advance so they can make arrangements
for transportation and housing.

If you notice from monthly reports sent from the Home
Office that your funds seem to be depleting faster at

home than they did overseas, it is probably due to the fact that your monthly allowance has been increased during your time of furlough. This means additional funds from deputation must be obtained to keep your account solvent.

Financial and medical clearance will be required before you will be allowed to prepare to return to the field. Close communication with the Home Office, therefore, is vital.

Some of these matters will seem trivial and unimportant. But so that the mission can carry on in a business-like manner, it is absolutely essential for each missionary to bear his part of the paper work. Don't let it discourage you.

21

Seeking New Workers

You will have many opportunities to be with and talk with people - Christian people - during your furlough time. It was once thought that if you wanted to interest workers in the field, you had to challenge high school and college-age young people. This is no longer true in the strictest sense. Missions are no longer looking only for the Bible College graduates. Men and women in their late 20's and 30's are now being sought to fill positions of need on the field. Short-term workers are found among young and old. Voluntary services are being rendered by countless numbers of retired individuals.

As a knowledgeable member of your Mission, and representative from your field, you will have, at your finger tips, a list of personnel needs. You will speak of these in your meetings and in your conversation with individuals. You will be able to explain the type of work which needs to be done. You will stand by your Mission and its policies, not condemning. You will emphasize to those who may be interested, that age is no longer an all-determining factor. Some missions have found older workers more ready and eager to adjust than some younger ones. They have not been severely handicapped by not learning the language in their younger years. And the very fact that they have several years of experience in their specialized training in the homeland can be of inestimable value on the field.

Young people are looking for a challenge. They do not expect an easy life. They are not looking for short cuts to a primrose path. They want to know that there is a place they can fill, a need for them as individuals and as Christian workers, and a task that they can do.

Perhaps as you talk with young people you will be amazed at their intelligent and academic approach to the matter of missions. Depending upon your own age and background, you may be shocked at the simplicity, reality, truthfulness and forthrightness of today's inquiring young man or woman. Nor will the length of the hair or the skirt determine for you if this is an interested inquirer who should be encouraged to approach your Board concerning service.

Young people are looking for reality in the world, and they are especially looking for it in you. No longer can you gloss over the hardships and even the mistakes missions have made. They want answers which are straight from the shoulder and true to fact. They are not interested in pretty Christian cliches. They are not primarily impressed with stories that have happy endings. They are little concerned with the material benefits and salary they may receive as long as there is a work for them to do, they are needed to do it, and they can find satisfaction in their role.

College young people today are going to expect certain things from you. They want to be heard. They have questions, and will expect you to have an awareness of their problems, and the issues which are vital concerns to them (social reform, race relations, new morality, war, the draft, etc.) They will also expect you to be fully apprised of the work of your own mission, the conditions (political, social, religious) in the country where you serve, your mission's strategy, your personal philosophy of missionary endeavor and the theological implications of ecumenicity. Although you may not be an intellectual or have expertise in the knowledge of world affairs, you will be expected to have and voice an opinion on a wide range of subjects. To today's young people, a missionary must be more than a dedicated worker who preaches the gospel of Jesus Christ.

The message you give to young people in seeking workers, must be Bible based, but related to things as they are. The matter of becoming personally involved in a cause which gives meaning to both the missionary and the work which he does cannot be stressed too much. You must be bold and honest in your approach. You will want to explain "old" and "common" Christian words in new ways so they lose none of their effectiveness, but are also meaningful to youth.

You have the possibility of seeking out a number of qualified workers for your agency. Some may be just now deciding on their life's work. Others may be finishing college and deciding what mission would best meet their needs. Some may be long out of school, but experienced in the pursuit of their profession. Others may have retired from business but still have a number of years of service to give to the Lord. Answer questions which are put to you and then be sure to emphasize the need for them to contact your Candidate or Personnel Secretary for full details and an application blank. Next to leading a soul to a saving knowledge of Jesus Christ, helping to turn a life toward the mission field is probably the greatest joy in life.

22

Additional Studies

Now that you have actually been in your missionary role and situation for a while, you are better able to determine the educational requirements demanded of you. Most of you went to the field with a minimum of one year of intensive Bible School training plus a minimal degree in your specialty because it was required by your Board. Now you find (1) the government of your host country demands a higher degree for you to continue to receive entry papers or (2) your work demands more extensive training in a specific field of knowledges and skills. You are not particularly impressed with the fact that you must study further, nor are you merely seeking additional letters after your name, but you realize the necessity for up-dating and furthering your educational capabilities. Continuing education (life-long learning) is a necessity in the day in which we live.

Let's take, for example, the case of an engineer working in communications media on the field. The store of scientific and technical knowledge and techniques involved in applying it have changed and expanded exceedingly rapidly in recent years. Most engineers find it very difficult to cope with these ever-increasing developments. Technological obsolescence is progressing at such a rate that retraining of engineers is imperative.

Although it seems reasonable that engineers could keep up with technological progress in their field through literature, we must take into account the fact

that there have been new breakthroughs in mathematics
and physics, and if the engineer is unfamiliar with
these new forms, he is not able to comprehend the
methodologies and technologies which are built there-
upon. Therefore, if an engineer does not understand
Matrix Algebra or Set and Ring Theory, for example,
he cannot keep up with his function. No longer can
men be fully trained for a lifetime of engineering
service.

If an engineer seeks to delve into Research and
Development, his needs for additional education will
be increased over those who are employed in Operations,
although the latter would need periodic refresher
courses in mathematics and/or the physical sciences.
If engineers do not keep pace with the forward move-
ment of their profession, they may be forced to
alter their role and become skilled technicians,
working under younger men who are better trained in
engineering. If the entire engineering staff suffers
from technical obsolescence, the work being done will
suffer from the same phenomenon, few new ideas will
be instituted and forward advance will be prohibitive.
Thus continual professional education must be the norm
for successful engineers and the advance of missionary
communication media.

Medicine is another field in which progress is so
rapidly producing new medicines, new surgical procedures, new techniques, that a doctor cannot hope to
keep up with his field. If he were a specialist and
could stay within the confines of his specialty, he
would have the benefits of his specialty magazines,
and taped series which are being produced constantly
to up-date him. But missionary doctors, in most field
situations, are general practitioners and/or general
surgeons, treating not only all kinds of diseases
and symptoms, but often having to deal with situations
in which they have had no prior training (leprosy,
elephantiasis, dysenteries, black water fever, etc.).
Time is limited for gaining knowledge through literature.

A nurse, too, finds she is ill-equipped for the
many-faceted responsibility of caring for patients.
She may be in a situation where she must undertake
minor surgical procedures, diagnose in place of a doctor,

supervise a training school for nurses, institute in-service programs, administrate a hospital, set up an intensive care unit, a cardiac unit or special care nursery, become an anesthetist or be involved in radiology. Some nurses will go to the field with a 3-year Nursing School R.N. background and others with a 4- or 5-year B.S. in Nursing Administration or Education. But with the shortage of staff, she is forced into situations beyond those in which she is knowledgeable and comfortable. She is forced to think in terms of additional training. In some cases, the host country is demanding more qualified nurses to take leadership roles in training and supervising national nurses.

Other professionals will find the same need for advanced or further training in their specialties. Missions are aware of the fact that if they are going to stay in competition, their workers must be as fully trained as possible. Technology from various parts of the world is filtering or flooding into smaller nations which were once interested in whatever small help the missionaries could give them. Today, help is more easily and readily available. Thus it is imperative that missionaries maintain the highest possible standards in every field, not only as a testimony to the Lord, but to uphold their place of respect in world evangelism.

Since more and more the place of the missionary is becoming that of one who trains national leadership, it is imperative that your knowledge be transmitted to qualified nationals. Thus, when the missionary arrives for furlough, there is a time of seeking God's will concerning further education, and you begin to ask some questions: What are my specific needs? Where and how can they be met? How long will it take? How much will it cost? Are refresher courses available? Will short seminars serve my purpose? Will working in my professional capacity in the homeland update me in processes and procedures sufficiently to prepare me for further service? Am I in a training capacity? Is my basic knowledge sufficient in the field in which I am engaged?

Some will feel the answer must be a leave of absence for educational purposes. Others will feel they are

highly enough qualified for their positions. Perhaps
one of the areas of missionary work which is most
neglected is that of administration. Very few men
and women in places of leadership have had training in
administration, counseling, inter-personal relations,
management, supervision, psychology, and other related
fields. There are excellent short courses, training
programs, and workshop-seminars being held throughout
the country today in these subject areas. Anyone
in a leadership role on the field should take advantage
of some means of understanding this role. Too long
untrained personnel have been given administrative
responsibilities without their roles and functions ever
being defined.

It is becoming increasingly more apparent that there
is a need for individuals who are adequately familiar with
and trained in such areas as anthropology, cross-cultural
studies, biblical and theological education by extension,
church growth, and all areas of communication. It would
be well to look into programs of this nature which are
offered by the Fuller School of World Mission, Missionary
Internship, the Billy Graham Communication Center at
Wheaton College, or other short-term courses, workshops,
and seminars in these fields.

Again, many things must be taken into consideration when thinking in terms of further education, whether
formal or informal learning. Your length of furlough,
home base, need for active deputation work, health
situation, family needs, as well as the needs of the
mission as a whole must be considered. Consider it
carefully. Pray about it. Discuss it with your
mission leaders, and act in the best interests of the
Lord's work through you, in your mission, on your
field.

23

Outfit Allowance And Purchases

Many Mission Boards have set guidelines concerning the amount of money which the returning missionary is allowed to spend on his equipment. Unfortunately, in too many cases, these allowances have not been revised periodically and thus the amounts listed are quite unrealistic when purchasing is begun.

As one who has been on the field, you are well aware of items which cannot be purchased there. You already have a supply of items which will not need to be replaced. (Some missionaries hold to the policy that they will sell all their goods to other missionaries before leaving the field. This means they can purchase everything new for their next term. It also means if they should, for some reason, not be able to return to the field, they would have no unfinished business there).

Except for items which are obsolete or not useful to you, those which would deteriorate during your absence, or those which are ready for replacement, it seems quite impractical to dispose of your material possessions. The price on all your items will have increased significantly. Duty on getting items into your field will be more difficult. Staying within your weight and financial limits set down by your Board for returning missionaries will cause hardships.

Many factors must be weighed. Will that 5-year old Jeep be good for another term, or should it be repaced? Should the reel-style tape recorder be sold so a more modern cassette-type can be purchased? Should the rather plain plastic dishes be replaced with a newer, prettier setting? Should a more expensive camera be purchased, or a movie camera to replace the 35mm? Should furniture be stored, loaned, or sold? Answers to these questions must be decided before leaving the field, but always with the consideration that replacement is expensive.

Clothing, unless hand-made at home, will be an exceedingly expensive item. Quality and cost must be carefully weighed before purchasing. Items essential in your work must then be considered (books, audio-visuals, tools, instruments, etc.). Household items which were lacking previously should then be considered. Finally, there should be those items which are non-essential, but important and time-saving.

There are discount houses and organizations available which obtain the best possible prices for missionaries needing equipment. Check with your Home Office if you do not know the names and addresses of these outlets. They can save you hundreds of dollars, depending on the items you must purchase. Take advantage of this program.

If you are purchasing items in general or clothing stores, be sure to ask about their discount policies. Many well-known stores give a 10-20% discount to Christian workers, but they may not advertise the fact. In some cities, your Mission Board will be allowed a discount for its workers as a non-profit organization.

In the event the store in which you intend to purchase items does NOT give a discount, do not demand one. They are under no obligation to do so. Remember that the owner's or manager's profits go down with each discount sale and then be grateful for those who are willing to do this, but also be understanding toward those who cannot limit themselves by this means.

Most missionaries find a church or group of individuals holding a shower of one type or another in order to provide necessary items for your return. If they

speak to you about this in advance, be sure to give them
at least this much information: (1) Plan the shower
no less than a month before your return to the field
so items can be packed adequately for shipment; (2) Give
them a list of items which would be most helpful to
you, in order of preference; (3) Supply a list of
items which are NOT needed or which are NOT allowed
into your country if there are restrictions; (4) Sizes
for each member of the family, if they are interested
in giving clothing.

When purchasing for your children, sizes will need
to be approximated for the length of your expected
term. This is, perhaps, one of the most difficult
tasks of all, but must be done if adequate clothing
and shoes are not available on your field.

Fortunately, in this day of increasing technology
with its supply and distribution, fields which once
could offer little or nothing of conveniences, clothing,
household goods and food which were considered
necessities in the homeland, are now being sold widely
and sometimes less expensively than items purchased in
the homeland. This is especially meaningful to missionaries.

Your outfit should be more easily produced upon your
return to the field than it was when you first left
the homeland. You know what you need and what you can
afford. You know what is available on your field.
Thus you can plan wisely and early - sometimes hitting
sales on needed items, sometimes mentioning needed
items in your newsletter and sometimes by the offers of
interested friends and churches.

Do think twice about some items. Is that freezer
or dishwasher essential or do you merely want to keep
up with or surpass your co-workers? Will those inexpensive dresses and shirts hold up under the rigors to
which they will be subjected, or would it prove less
expensive to pay for better quality?

Many of you have found that being encumbered with
a great amount of material possessions has been a hin-
drance to you and your work. Perhaps this is especially

true of those who live and work down country or in the
bush.   Others have found that for your ministry among
the higher classes of people in your city, you need
more material possessions than you had anticipated.
Thus one cannot fairly estimate for another what items
are essential.   But you can determine this fairly and
honestly for yourself.   God will supply all your need,
so look to Him to fulfill His promise to you.

24

Packing And Shipping

Moving will no longer be a new experience for you. It is possible, however, that a few details have been forgotten since you packed before leaving for the field last time.

Since you will have a better knowledge of what you need to take back to the field, you can better plan on how many containers will need to be found or purchased to accommodate your baggage. You will choose your containers according to the method by which your excess baggage is to be shipped. Stronger, heavier containers may be used if it is to go by sea. Lighter fiber barrels and foot lockers may be utilized if items are to be airlifted. Convenience and cost will usually determine the method of shipping. Although most baggage is now containerized you may want to pack foot lockers or fiber barrels in order to use them for storage on the field.

In packing, remember that the pieces of luggage you take with you should contain sufficient supplies to maintain you until your other items arrive. In the event of plane or dock strikes, considerable delay may result in obtaining necessary clothing or toilet articles.

You may wish to commit your equipment to a packing company. Keep in mind the cost, however. Then, too, if you are shipping by air, don't allow the company to use heavy crating or steel barrels. Some items may be ordered from stores which cater to overseas shipping. Give accurate details as to how items should be addressed and sent by them.

It is good to pack several types of items in each container, i.e., some clothing, some bedding, some books, some kitchen utensils, etc. In the event a container should be lost or delayed, you will not suffer the loss of all you have of one item.

Be sure each container is well identified. Make a list of the items in each piece of luggage, and be sure the number on your list corresponds with the identically numbered container. When listing items for customs, do not list each separate sock or shirt. Lump items by categories. For insurance purposes, however, an itemized listing is essential. For customs purposes, list the fair wholesale value of the items. For insurance purposes, list the replacement value.

Clothing should be worn and/or laundered before being packed, and thereby conform to the category of used clothing.

If large items of equipment will need an import license, be sure to apply for it well ahead of your departure date. (Pianos, cars, trucks, organs, etc., usually require special papers).

You will want to find out the quickest, easiest and best way of transporting your goods to the port of embarkation. For some it may mean hiring a trailer to pull behind your car. For others it will be a Trucking Company, Moving Van Company, plane, bus or Railway Express. Time is of an essence as well as the expense involved. So check carefully and choose wisely.

If your items are sent to the plane or dock, be sure your forwarding address is clearly indicated on each piece. A letter must always be sent, stating how many pieces will arrive, the approximate arrival date, and explicit instructions should be given as to how, when and where the shipment is to be sent. If additional pieces are to be added from stores, packers, or by you at a later date, be sure to indicate this. If the same shipper is used by all members of your mission you will find a very helpful agent to make matters go smoothly.

If your shipment is going by air and your field of

service requires that you actually be in that country before your items arrive, be careful to plan your shipment date carefully, especially if you are not planning to go directly to your field of service.

Make sure your insurance coverage is sufficient to cover any loss you may sustain in the homeland or in transit overseas. Carry your bill of lading, including insurance coverage, with you.

You will probably be asked to transport various and sundry items to the field for the mission and/or fellow missionaries. This should be only with your permission and prior written approval.

When you arrive on the field, be sure to state to customs officials the exact number of pieces to arrive as unaccompanied baggage, when they are expected, and by what means they will reach you.

Securely lock each item being sent. Steel bands may also be utilized as well as spot welding covers on fibre and steel barrels. If a vehicle is being sent, it is good to remove windshield wipers, mirrors, hubcaps, and other such items. Lock the spare tire in or on the vehicle, and lock the hood. It is amazing how many pieces can disappear (fan belt, battery, gas tank cover, etc.) if not securely "tied down".

You know from previous experience that items of personal or intrinsic value can be broken, lost or stolen at any time. Be glad for all that you have, but if any or all of your material things should be taken from you, be content in the knowledge that even then, God is able to make all grace abound toward you and HE will supply all your need in Christ Jesus.

25

Early Furlough, Extended Furlough And Leave Of Absence

The happy candidate goes to the field filled with the excitement of first term missionary-itis and the expectation of serving a lifetime on the field of God's choice. Many find that dream fulfilled.

In the course of human events, however, there are trials, disappointments, delays, the unexpected, as well as the joys and happinesses, encouragements and reached goals. And there are times when missionaries must come to grips with factors beyond their control. Often the result must be a forced furlough - coming home sooner than anticipated. It is not an occasion of joy, but one of sadness in most cases. Among the most common reasons for early furlough are:

1. Debilitating sickness or accident

2. Psychological factors

3. Illness or death of a relative in the homeland

4. Needs of young people in the family

5. Proper rotation of missionary staff

6. Government restrictions

7. War, riots or rebellions

8. Discipline measures

9.   Need for help in the Home Office

10.   Settlement of business or legal matters.

For these and other reasons, missionaries must, often hurriedly, make arrangements to leave the country. He is burdened with the pressures of leaving his work unfinished as well as the cares of whatever is forcing him to go to the homeland. It is a distressing period, draining the physical, mental and emotional stability of the missionary. His spiritual strength is lessened as time is compressed and there is so much to do, so many worries, the unknown of the future. It ought not to be, but we ARE still human and God understands this even when we and our associates condemn it.

It is at times like these that God has an oppor- tunity to prove Himself to us. He, of course, was aware of these events from the beginning. They came as no surprise to Him. But what is your reaction? Does your attitude show an implicit and unmoveable faith in the God of Job ("Though He slay me, yet will I trust in Him" Job 13:15)? Do the "Whys?" and "Hows?" overpower the knowledge that "He knoweth the way that I take: when he hath tried me, I shall come forth as gold" (Job 23:10).

Although the human heart cry is for sympathy, our strength and satisfaction must be found in the fact that "Even the Son of man came not to be ministered unto, but to minister, and to give his life a ransom for many" (Mark 10:45).

Few will understand your heartache, the turmoil raging within you, the tears, the frustration. But if God is not Lord of all, He is not Lord at all. He is sufficient, in truth. These are the days to find out the reality of His promises. No matter what is taken from you, nothing can separate you from the love of God. Yes, the LOVE of God. He has not brought this trial to you in His wrath. There was no other way He could have caused you to grow and mature. You may not be able to comprehend His secret just now, but as He brings you through this darkened tunnel, you will be able to see the light on the other side. It may take time, patience and sheer persistence. But He means it for your good - whatever it is.

> What better way to thank my Lord
> For the life that He has lent,
> Than in whatsoever state I am,
> Therewith to be content.

And, dear missionary friend, if such a trial has not been entrusted to you, be grateful. But also be very understanding of those who must face such situations. They need your love and support as never before. Do what you can to help them through their night of depression and desperation. They may not ask for your help; in fact, they may show very little appreciation for it at the time. But be assured they need a friend who cares enough to be concerned. Just standing by can be of tremendous value.

Then there are those who, having been home on furlough, find that their return to the field must be delayed. The reasons for this are varied, also. Some of them include:

1. Inability to obtain financial clearance

2. Inability to obtain medical clearance

3. Care of aging parents

4. Problems related to your young people

5. Uncertainty as to God's leading

6. Visa unobtainable

7. Adoption of a child

8. Request by the Home Office for special service (administration, deputation or representation)

It may be a disappointment to see your anticipated date of departure for return to the field delayed. But God sometimes allows responsibilities to come into the life, unexpectedly, and they must be cared for as diligently as the work on the field. One's own health and family must be given prime consideration. Many single women find themselves at home for many years, tied down with the care of ill and/or aging parents. Married

couples find themselves with a rebellious teenager who
feels his mother and dad think more of the mission field
than they do of him. Visas for several countries of
the world are becoming increasingly difficult to obtain.
Parents who arrange for an adoption usually must be in
the homeland for a period of not less than a year. With
a shortage of workers at home, furlough folks are sometimes asked to assume mission responsibilities in the
homeland for a year or two, or longer. Thus furloughs
must be extended to cover such emergencies and exigencies.

To some it is apparent after a 3 or 6 month extension
of furlough that a leave of absence is necessary. Obtaining this status allows the missionary to maintain
a relationship with the mission so that a resignation is not necessary. Certain benefits may be kept active (e.g., retirement fund, health insurance). In
most instances, however, payment of housing and allowance,
insurance, travel, etc., cannot be continued beyond a
limited period of time set by the mission and strictly
stated in its By-laws or policies. It does mean that
any funds which come in designated for your account are
credited properly and your account is built up for the
time when you may be able to resume your missionary work
on the field. Some missionaries take a leave of
absence during the time their children are in high
school, especially if there is no secondary school education available on the field. Education during furlough may require a leave of absence, or an extended
time limit. Physical condition may necessitate a leave.
Some want time to reconsider their whole missionary
commitment. Most missions are lenient about allowing
a leave of absence if they feel you are sincere and
they want to preserve your service for the mission.

Certain facts must be faced if you decide on a leave
of absence. Ordinarily, support from the Board will
not be available. Thus you will be responsible for
earning your livelihood through other work. This may
be a very real concern if you must care for someone
who is ill, for you will not be free to go out and
find work. God, however, has a way of meeting your
need, although you cannot see it now. It may be through
your family, an agency, or friends. He will work in
each situation and make provision.

A leave of absence may cause you to feel as if you are in "no-man's land", being neither a missionary or anything else for the time being. People may have questions if they ask "What is your work?" and you reply, "I'm a missionary on leave of absence". An explanation as to the reasons for such leave is probably in order.

As soon as plans have been completed, the problem has been worked out, or the crisis has passed, change your status with the mission. Keep in close contact with the Home Office at all times, informing them of your progress and keeping up on news from your field. In most missions, a leave of absence status must be voted upon annually. If they vote against granting the LOA for an additional period of time, you will be asked to submit your resignation.

Early furloughs, extended furloughs and leaves of absence make adjustments in the field staff necessary. Therefore, it is important that they be taken only when no other solution can be found to problems which present themselves to you, and be terminated as quickly as possible and feasible.

26

Changing Missions During Furlough

There are circumstances brought to bear upon certain missionaries which necessitate his becoming connected with a mission other than the one with which he was originally affiliated. There are many reasons for this. We will discuss but a few. But no matter the reason, it is always best for this change to take place during the furlough period so that official matters can be legally finalized and supporters can be informed, in person, of this new association.

1. You marry, or plan to marry a member of another mission working in your field. Most often it is the girl who joins the fellow's mission, but occasionally the opposite is true. This is, obviously, an uncomplicated reason for changing missions.

2. You have been loaned to another mission during your term of service. Having become involved in that work, you feel you could become a more vital part of it if you were to become a member of that mission rather than continuing on loan to them.

3. You may feel led to assume a specific ministry in which your mission has not felt led to enter (e.g., orphanage work, Bible Training School, film ministry). A sister mission is willing to allow you to assume this special work. Some

missions also set rules as to where single
girls can work and where they feel the ministry
should be carried on by a man or married couple.
This may be true if a girl wants to work in
an isolated tribal area or an especially
dangerous zone. Another mission may not put
restrictions upon their members.

4. After a term on the field, you may become
    increasingly concerned with another area where
    you feel your abilities can be better utilized.
    There may be no change in language, but your
    present mission does not work in that area.

5. Closing of a field due to government or
    mission controls and restrictions may cause
    you to seek another field under another Board.

6. You have found good Christian fellowship with
    members of another mission. Your inter-personal
    relations with your own fellow-missionaries
    have fallen short of expectations. You feel
    a happier situation will exist if you join
    the other group.

7. Doctrinal problems may arise which will serve
    to direct you to another Board. It may be that
    your group has become liberal, or involved in
    tangent doctrines, or perhaps it is you who
    have changed in these directions, but you
    still want to serve in your chosen field.

8. Denominational missions, because of lack of
    funds, may cut down on the number of mission-
    aries in a given field, or close the field
    entirely. Some of these missionaries will
    apply for service with other Boards.

9. Maybe you just don't like your Board now that
    you have come to see it at close range. You
    don't like the authority. You have no freedom
    to go or say or be or do. Rules and regulations
    tie your hands as you seek to serve. You thought
    the situation could be worked out, but there
    seems to be no common ground. Another mission
    appears to be, if not utopian, at least more
    to your liking.

10. You may be requested not to return with your
     Board because of actions or attitudes. But
     you insist upon returning and you find a mission,
     who in spite of your history, accepts you for
     further service.

Before changing missions, you must remember that no
organization is perfect. Each one has its own unique
problems, sometimes undetected from the outside.

Also consider the fact that returning to the same
field under a different mission will cause many
questions to be raised, especially if you return to
the same approximate area to do a similar work as
previously. If your mission adheres to comity, you
will not likely be serving at the same down-country
station, but it IS possible that you will be in the
same city (which may be "open" with no comity rules).
Nationals will ask for an explanation. Your former
co-workers will be full of questions. Rumors will
spread. Therefore, it is essential that you be
strongly convicted by the Lord that you are in His
best will. Never condemn or criticize your former
work, especially to nationals. Don't blame a mission
or a co-worker for that which has taken place in your
life. Your call to a different mission must be as certain as the Lord's call upon your life for service. Once
convinced yourself, you will be able to share this with
others.

Since missions, as a rule, work very closely with
one another, your past performance will be considered
carefully before you are accepted by another group. In
most cases, a missionary does not simply transfer from
one mission to another. Usually a mission will not
consider the application of an individual who already
is a member of another group. This means, then, that
you must resign from your previous membership before
beginning your new candidate procedure. Often you will
be required to attend Candidate School and follow all
procedures required of other prospective candidates.
And it is even possible you may be rejected after due
consideration by the Board.

There are truly legitimate and wise reasons for
changing missions. There are also very immature, selfish

and unworthy reasons for doing so. Determine, with
God's approval, to accomplish His highest and best
in and through your life. He will give light for your
pathway as you seek Him with all your heart and mind.

27

Suppose Your Field Closes
During Furlough

There is little need to emphasize the uncertainty of the days in which we live. Nations are rising against nation, and in many parts of the world it is difficult to determine how long missionaries may be allowed entry into certain countries.

What steps should you take if your field of service closes while you are on furlough? Here are some of the alternatives:

1. Wait two or three years to see if the doors will open to missionary service once again. This has happened in many fields.

2. Give up foreign missionary work and stay in the homeland as a worker in the Home Office, or as a Regional Representative for the Mission.

3. Determine that you will go into secular work in the homeland.

4. Decide to be a missionary at home by working in a ghetto, coffee house, or as a Christian Education Director or Youth Director or Church Secretary.

5. Take a church at home.

6. Volunteer for another field in which your mission works where you can use your present language.

7. Volunteer for a field where a different
    language is used.

8. Apply to a different Board for another field.

9. Destroy your effectiveness in any future
    ministry by tenaciously holding to something
    that can never be.

It is no light thing to be told you are not welcome
to return to a country or a people whom you have come
to know and love, especially when your whole life has
been aimed toward that specific field and people.

If you decide to wait a while to see if the doors
will open again, it may be that your support will be
dropped after several months at home. You will, undoubtedly, have to work until such time as you can
return to the field, or the field seems definitely
unreachable for you.

If an entire field closes, your mission may not be
able to put you on the payroll at home. If, however,
there are few people involved, they may be able to use
some extra hands in the office or in deputational
ministry.

Some will feel this action was ordained of God and
a sign that they should seek work in the secular
field, perhaps to earn money in order to support
missions and other Christian works.

There is a great deal of Christian work to be done
in the homeland. There will be little difficulty in
locating a satisfying ministry.

Men who have been ordained may decide to pastor
a church in the homeland, by which means they can emphasize missions and interest young people in Christian
work. Having had experience on the field should make
them prepared to promote this aspect of the church to a
large extent.

If you accept an appointment to another field in
which your Board operates, and the same language you
have learned for your first appointment is used, there

is less adaptation needed. The people may have different culture, mores, customs; the country may be desert instead of mountainous; the work may be more or less advanced than your former field. But at least you will be able to communicate with the people - and the rest comes far easier.

If you decide on a completely new field of service, you will have to consider yourself to be a "new" missionary all over again. Although many fine workers have done this very thing, it is always difficult not to say, "When I was in _____, we did it such and such a way," expecting because it worked there, it will work the same way here. It will take time to learn the new language and become acquainted with the country and its people. You may become very frustrated if the people are opposite to your former contacts. Perhaps you came from a spiritually fruitful field; this one is barren. Previously you were in charge of a station; now you are not even consulted in decisions concerning your own ministry. Did you make the wrong decision? Or can these problems be worked out to such an advantage that you will come to love this field as much or better than your first? To a large extent YOU will determine the answer.

Perhaps your Board has no work in a field in which you have a particular concern. It would then be in order to consider joining a Board which works in the areas of your interest. If this second Board is of the same calibre as your previous affiliation, most, if not all of your supporters will continue to send you forth.

Some will feel that their whole life and ministry has gone down the drain if the door closes to their field. They bemoan this irreversible fact so greatly that it adversely affects any other work they may decide to do. Thus their lives become wasted and useless. It, of course, comes as a shock and disappointment. But it comes as no surprise to the God whom you serve. You can, therefore, be confident that He has good, acceptable, and perfect reasons for these seeming impossibilities.

The choice now is whether this is a call for you to

look to another field of service, or an open door for
you to enter a different sphere of ministry. The
most important responsibility is to be faithful to
Him wherever you choose to serve.

It may be a more complicated and difficult situation if you are under a Board which has determined
that for safety purposes, or because of increasing
tension with nationals in the administering and
carrying out of the work, or because of prohibitions
against openly preaching the Word, they must close that
field. Another mission or missions have decided to
stay in the land. Do you quit your mission and go
with another? Do you try to get involved with a health,
education or government agency working in that country?
Do you storm the gates of your administrative board
and accuse them of making a wrong decision? How you
act, react and interact in such a situation can be the
making or breaking of your Board as well as of you as
an individual missionary.

In this day of ever-changing political positions,
we may see more and more missionaries being refused
re-entry permits and visaes. If, on the other hand,
doors to your work are wide open, prepare to return
and be grateful for further opportunity with your people.
Plan well, for there may come a day when YOU will have
to face the unhappy situation of not being able to
return.

28

Resignation

If you have come home with the thought that you are through as a missionary, furlough is a good time to work it out and get it straight. Refresh yourself for several weeks. Pray unceasingly. Share your thoughts and feelings with your closest friends and prayer partners in the most unbiased way possible. Arrange for a conference at the Home Office and bring up the problems you are facing. Gain expert advise from those who are neutral in the situation but perceptive in their thinking. If your health or a family situation is the problem, allow time to see if it can be worked out satisfactorily. Perhaps an extended furlough or leave of absence will solve the problem for you. In any case, your furlough is a time of special consideration of God's call upon your life. Be very sure Satan does not blind you to the perfect will of God.

If, after due consideration, and an honest leading from the Lord, you feel you must resign from the Mission, be sure to take care of all necessary details with your Home Office. Decide with them whether you or they should write your supporters. Often support is salvaged for another missionary if the supporting church or individuals are contacted in a way which gives them an opportunity to transfer their support to another missionary or a project in which you are especially involved or interested.

Supporters are usually very lenient in their feelings toward those who resign because of personal or
family health problems, inability to adjust to the
demands placed upon you, a take-over of the work by
nationals or expulsion from the country for reasons
beyond your control (even though you might be able
to go to another area or country under the same
mission). They are less lenient of those who become
embittered, speak disparagingly of the work, the
country, the nationals, the mission, or decide they
can be happier or make more money in the homeland.
Fortunately, most supporters never know when their
missionary has been requested to turn in his resignation
because of bad attitudes, open sin, or pressure from
fellow-missionaries who feel they could work in harmony
apart from this individual. Reversals or changes
in doctrine resulting in resignations must be carefully considered by the individual and the Mission.
In some cases the missionary will not feel he can
work any longer within the restrictions of his Board's
statement of faith. In other cases, the missionary
feels no constraint to resign, but is forced to do
so because his views are not those firmly established
by his Board. In recent times the biggest problem in
the area of doctrine has been the question of healing,
speaking in tongues, the view of the Holy Spirit and
the social implications of the Gospel. A most unsatis-
factory answer is where a Board says "You can believe
it, but you can't practice or teach it," and the individual is allowed to remain in the Mission.

A missionary should be truthful, but in many cases,
the truth concerning a resignation is very one-sided
and therefore strongly biased. Condemning a mission
for a few isolated and unintentional instances is
hardly fair. Although you may not have found your
niche with the Board, or feel you have been treated
unfairly, others have found a very happy relationship
serving under the same Board. There is always the
possibility that you were responsible in a slight way
for the dissolution of your affiliation. At any rate,
it is always best to tell the brightest side of the
true story.

For those who find they must resign for acceptable
and legitimate reasons, have you looked into the

possibility of serving your Board in the homeland –
as a Special Representative, Home Office worker,
Deputationist, Regional Secretary?

There may be some who even now are undecided about
the future. The facts seem to indicate that resignation
is the best answer. But you are beset with fears:
What will the Board think? How will my home church
feel? How can I explain to my supporters? What will
it do to my children? Isn't my faith enough to get
me through another term? Is it better that I live out
my few remaining days on the field with the possibility
my illness will increase and other workers will need
to care for me? What will I do if I stay home?

There is really only one answer to your problem.
It comes by laying the facts on the table, evaluating
the pros and cons, obtaining the best advice possible
and committing your decision to the Lord before, between
and at the end of your prayerful deliberations. He
will show you *His* answer. Once you have made your
decision and are assured that the reasons for it are
valid, stick by it. There is no need to go back and
worry about it. Making the right choice and being
sure of it are far more important than wondering what
people may think of you for what you have done.

29

Return To The Field

The weeks and months have flown. Is it possible you've travelled so many miles to conduct meetings? You still marvel at God's supply of every need, in spite of the fact you had prayed unceasingly for this to be true. Every bill has been paid. Equipment has been purchased, packed and forwarded for shipment. Shots and immunizations have been obtained. Medical clearance has been received. Social calls have come to an end. Most problems have been solved, questions answered, and personal needs met.

Adjustment to the homeland was difficult, but at least you were able to cope. You appreciated the hospitality and comforts which friends provided for you. You're grateful for renewed fellowship with supporters and the opportunity to speak in places where you and your mission had not previously been known. There were many along the way who seemed to be interested in learning more about applying for service. There were occasions when special ministries were honored with spiritual results. Souls were saved and built up in the faith for you were no less a missionary just because you had returned to the home-land for furlough.

Perhaps your children began to get a taste for material things. They may miss some of the niceties of life when they return to the field. Or, on the other hand, they may look forward to returning to the field and to their friends who better understand them.

It is never easy to say farewell to those whom you dearly love. Perhaps you must leave a Mother or Dad still unsaved, or secure in Christ but physically incapacitated. Or for the first time, your family will be separated as you leave a son or daughter in the homeland to enter a Christian School or College. You know you must be strong in the Lord and you're assured that His grace is sufficient. But these are difficult hours.

Yet, in spite of the heart ties and cries, you are looking forward to another term of service, determined by the grace of God to be a more effective witness, a more mature counselor, a more loving co-worker, a more obedient steward of talents and time, a more fully informed administrator, a more faithful child of God.

No one can be sure how much time he will have to work in his field. Plans must be carried out as quickly as possible to meet goals which have been set. Nationals must be trained and given authority and a voice in decisions. There must be more teamwork between missionary and missionary, between missionary and national, between your mission and other missions, between the Field Office and the Home Office. You are a vital part of this program of advance, and there is much to do. And there is no assurance how long is left to you for doing it.

So with "Goodbye" and "God bless you" ringing in your ears, you head through the gate and board your plane. As you taxi to the end of the runway, then speed ahead faster and faster until you hear and feel the wheels leave the pavement and fold themselves under your feet, you take a last look at the homeland, grateful for the opportunity you've had of returning for this short while, knowing it will be greatly changed before you see it again, but anxiously awaiting your arrival on the field to take up the work to which God has led you. And whether you return to the exact location of your previous term, or are assigned to another station and work in a different area, you will be grateful that you are a co-laborer with God in the soul-satisfying ministry of missionary endeavor.

Miss Marjorie A. Collins has a B.A. in Bible and Missions. She writes from personal experience in the fields of Missions and Christian Education. She was a missionary to Pakistan, a Christian Education Director, and for several years, Personnel Secretary for The W.R.M.F., Inc. (HCJB). She presently serves on the Board of OCEAN, Inc. (a missionary organization providing continuing education for American nurses serving overseas) and is involved not only as a free-lance writer and author, but is a teacher of Creative Writing and Teaching Assistant to President J. Robertson McQuilkin of Columbia Bible College and Columbia Graduate School of Bible and Missions in Columbia, South Carolina.

As of this writing, Miss Collins has had over 400 articles published in various Christian magazines. She is also the author of several books, including *Manual for Accepted Missionary Candidates* (William Carey Library), *Who Cares About the Missionary?* (Moody Press), and *Dedication: What It's All About* (Bethany Fellowship).